Mark Bryant DeWitt
15 La Cuesta Road
Orinda, CA 94563
United States of America

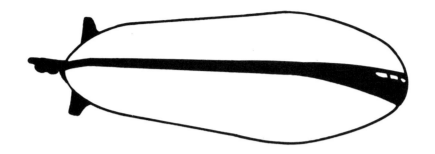

AIRSHIPS for the FUTURE

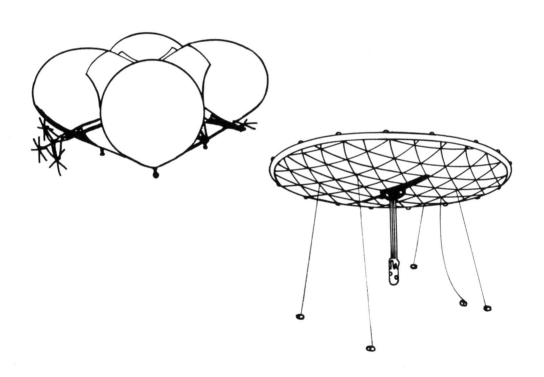

AIRSHIPS
for the FUTURE

By WILLIAM J. WHITE

STERLING PUBLISHING CO., INC.   NEW YORK
Oak Tree Press Co., Ltd.
London & Sydney

OTHER BOOKS OF INTEREST

Air Facts & Feats

Car Facts & Feats

To Gabe
who happened to be the right guy
in the right place
at the right time.

Revised Edition

Third Printing, 1979

Copyright © 1978, 1976 by Sterling Publishing Co., Inc.
Two Park Avenue, New York, N.Y. 10016
Distributed in Australia by Oak Tree Press Co., Ltd.,
P.O. Box J34, Brickfield Hill, Sydney 2000, N.S.W.
Distributed in the United Kingdom
by Ward Lock Ltd., 116 Baker Street, London W.1
Manufactured in the United States of America
All rights reserved
Library of Congress Catalog Card No.: 76-19768
Sterling ISBN 0-8069-0090-3 Trade   Oak Tree 7061-2502-9
0091-1 Library

contents

Environmental airships of the future at work. Sounding balloons and rockets are launched from the top, while radiometric sensors on the bottom collect scientific data. The airship is equipped to lower and recover submersibles and buoys and also for hook-on and release of aircraft. The airship at bottom is engaged in cleaning up an oil slick.

6

introduction

On the evening of May 6, 1937 at Lakehurst, New Jersey, the great and majestic airship *Hindenburg* came to a fiery end after completing a beautiful cruise from Europe. Thirty-five lives were lost and taps were played for the airship industry. The industry was young, and the political problems surrounding it turned the crash into an all-consuming holocaust.

At 4:06 P.M. on June 24, 1975, Flight 66, an Eastern Airlines Boeing 727 out of New Orleans was coming in for a routine landing at New York's Kennedy Airport when wind shear caught it and the big jetliner slammed down into the approach lights, killing 113 people. This was the single greatest disaster in American aviation history, but instead of playing taps for the airline industry, a multitude of experts began corrective procedures to preclude further accidents.

The holocaust in New York did not produce cries to abandon the aircraft industry, the way the commercial airship industry was knocked out by the *Hindenburg* disaster. The airship industry has been dormant for 40 years, but today there are signs that the airship will rise again, providing the answer to some of our most perplexing problems. The plans are already well underway, but to understand where the airship is heading, an appreciation of some background and history is in order.

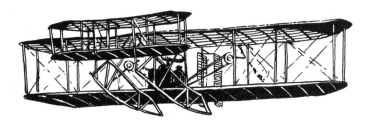

Man's first successful flight occurred in 1783 when Jean François Pilâtre de Rozier and the Marquis d'Arlandres ascended in an untethered hot-air balloon constructed by the Montgolfier brothers. Heavier-than-air flight did not get off the ground until the Wright brothers' flight in 1903.

This huge hangar in Friedrichshafen, Germany, sheltered the airship "Los Angeles" before its delivery to the U.S.

We must understand the basics of lighter-than-air travel and look briefly at the efforts of the airship pioneers who brought us our first taste of flight 120 years before the Wright brothers took off at Kitty Hawk. We will examine the glorious era of airship aviation when people soared through the skies in chariots nearly three times as long as a football field, where passengers slept in comfortable berths or whiled away the hours in luxurious staterooms. These great zeppelins contained special smoking lounges with electric cigarette lighters, many-volumed libraries with hotel-style writing desks, spacious salons for dancing and drinking and a dining room larger than those on Pullman trains. There were classical recitals on a grand piano and nearly 100 yards (90 metres) of promenade decks which offered a thrilling view through tilted panoramic windows of the earth 3,000 feet (900 metres) below.

On the ground, the hangars for the airships were built so large that clouds formed inside them and it began to rain inside while the sun shone brightly overhead. The safety record was amazing for the number of passenger miles flown. The few dramatic crashes, however, along with a growing demand for speed, forced the airship era to give way to the airplane.

In the Thirties it may have seemed like a good idea to abandon the airship. However, the Seventies ushered in an era of turmoil. The world awakened to the fact that there is an energy shortage. Environmentalists and ecologists raised a cry that the energy seekers are ruining the natural beauty of the earth and endangering the world's wildlife. Automobiles and huge airliners poison the very air we breathe while the noise they cause may be affecting the hearing of generations to come.

The price of energy, including electricity, oil, natural gas and coal has streaked out of sight. Auto makers battle to increase miles-per-gallon while trying to meet governmental pollution standards. Some experiment with radical changes, bringing back the electric or steam car or sharply modifying the internal combustion engine.

The government is underwriting the operation of the major airlines because they alone cannot cope with high operating costs and smaller passenger loads. The price of fuel for aircraft has quadrupled in a year and a half from about 11 cents a gallon to 50 cents a gallon, forcing the airlines to increase their passenger fares. They realize, though, that fares have already reached the point of diminishing returns.

Scientists are doggedly trying to come up with some way to stem the tide. Many believe the best solution is to bring back the airship. Some estimates say 10 to 15 small, effective airships could be built for the price of one jumbo jetliner. For $22,000,000 as opposed to $30,000,000 for a jumbo jet with a payload of 86 tons (78 tonnes), an airship could be built with a cargo potential of 1,000 tons (900 tonnes) which could travel at 200 miles (320 kilometres) per hour. It would not pollute the air and would make practically no noise at all. It would be three times as cheap to operate as an airplane and would not need the massive airports that now dot the country, causing thousands of complaints from irate citizens. Eighteen hundred passengers could make the trip from a pier or other open space

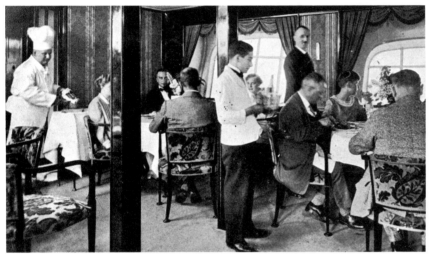

Dinner aboard the "Graf Zeppelin" was a luxurious experience featuring fine wines and gourmet cuisine.

in New York Harbor to a pier in San Francisco in under 24 hours at a cost of less than $50, or float down to Washington in under 3 hours for less than the cost of a bus ticket. The airship of the future would be faster than buses or trains and more efficient than airplanes.

The trucking industry has for all practical purposes taken over the rail-road cargo business and the airplane has taken over the passenger service. The airship has the potential to take over much of the gas-consuming long-haul trucking commerce and put a substantial hole in the gas-consuming airline passenger service. Not only will the airship be able to offer improved cost, but more efficient and, in many cases faster, service.

The airship industry has been sleeping since the Thirties, but the combination of the energy shortage, pollution and the tremendous cost of transportation has provided the right climate for an immediate awakening. The airships will now stretch their ballonets, leave their moorings and, with 40 years of new technology at their service, take their place once again as a top mode of peaceful transportation in the modern world.

Airships have long been a highlight of public celebrations. At left, the airship contingent at the Hudson-Fulton Celebration in New York, 1909 and below, the Goodyear blimp at Operation Sail, July 4, 1976 in New York Harbor.

the basics

WHAT ARE THEY?

The word "airship" doesn't have an air of romance or excitement for most people. It doesn't bring a vivid picture to mind. But say the word "blimp" and the average person thinks of the distinctive shape of the Goodyear blimp hanging as if by magic in the sky overhead. The word "dirigible" or "zeppelin" brings to mind images of a huge metal-hulled ship soaring over the German countryside.

Yet the general term for the blimps and zeppelins of the past and the shapes and sizes of the future is AIRSHIP, "a form of mechanically driven aircraft, lighter-than-air, having a means of controlling the direction of its motion" as defined in Webster's International Dictionary. The field of lighter-than-air flight is basically divided into two categories, the balloons and the airships. Often the shapes and materials are similar, but an airship can move when and where it is needed, while a balloon is at the mercy of the winds. DIRIGIBLE is another commonly used name for lighter-than-air craft, having virtually the same meaning as "airship."

There are three basic types of airship: non-rigid, rigid and semi-rigid. The non-rigids, or blimps, are the only airships flying today. Many of the great airships of the past, including the *Graf Zeppelin* and the *Hindenburg,* were rigids. A ZEPPELIN is a rigid airship of the type first constructed by Count von Zeppelin, the pioneering German manufacturer, in 1899–1900. Airships are also designed as semi-rigid, combining the basic characteristics of the non-rigids with some rigid supporting structure.

The airship, unlike the airplane, does not depend on the expenditure of fuel to get its lift. This leads to a great saving in fuel consumption when compared with a DC-8, for instance, which requires the consumption of approximately 60,000 pounds (27,250 kilograms) of fuel for a 5-hour flight. During the first 30 minutes, the time it takes to reach cruising altitude, the plane will burn 10,000 pounds (4,550 kilograms) of fuel. That is, almost 17 per cent of the fuel is consumed during the lifting portion of the flight, comprising only 10 per cent of the time in the air and an even smaller percentage of the distance traveled. By avoiding the battle with gravity, the airship saves tremendous quantities of expensive fuel.

(A glossary of technical terms can be found in the back of this book.)

THE LIFTING GASES

Three gases have been used to provide lift for airships in the past, and even the most advanced airship designers have limited their exploration to ships filled with hydrogen, helium or hot air, all of which will rise in the atmosphere. While hot air has been used extensively in sport ballooning and has now been adapted for use in hot-air airships (see pages 122–126), the greatest commercial potential rests with hydrogen or helium, and of these helium is clearly preferred.

Hydrogen is 10 per cent better for lifting weight than helium. It exists in inexhaustible quantities and is extremely cheap to produce. However, it is highly inflammable. The greatest disaster in airship history, the explosion of the *Hindenburg,* occurred because the German government could not acquire helium and had to employ hydrogen in their zeppelins. This famous crash has traditionally been blamed for the decline of the airship industry, and there is little chance that the public would accept a hydrogen-filled airship with the image of burning wreckage firmly planted in their minds. In fact, by making use of the technological advances which have occurred between the 1930's and the present, hydrogen could be made just as safe to use as gasoline for automobiles or jet fuel for jumbo airliners. Nevertheless, unless scientists and engineers can break the fear syndrome surrounding the use of hydrogen, airships of the future will be designed with the use of helium in mind.

Helium is a colorless, odorless, tasteless, nonpoisonous, noncombustible gaseous element. It belongs to a family of rare gases, and is found in the atmosphere, in gases from mineral springs, in mines, volcanoes and sea water. It is present in nearly all rocks and minerals but in very small quantity, usually one part in 200,000. Some natural gases contain one to eight per cent helium, and this is the only known source where large quantities can be extracted at a reasonable cost.

Until recently, large concentrations of these gases had been discovered only in some fields in the United States and Canada, principally in Texas, Kansas, Colorado, Utah, New Mexico, Ontario and Alberta. However, the U.S. lost its virtual monopoly on helium with the discovery of helium sources in Russia and Poland. Not much is known at this point concerning the quantity involved, but it is known that Poland is exporting the lifting gas. A New Jersey firm has contracted with the Polish ministry to import helium from Poland and sell it internationally. There are also unsubstantiated reports of airship construction, including heavy-lift vehicles, in the U.S.S.R.

Since helium is second only to hydrogen in lifting power, the U.S. began

Hydrogen gas for the "Hindenburg" is prepared for shipment.

volume production in 1917 for use in observation balloons. The method used for extracting the helium from natural gas is liquefaction. Carbon dioxide and water vapor (which solidifies in the process) are first removed chemically, then the gas is cooled to a temperature below that at which all its constituents except helium are liquefied.

The sale and export of government-produced helium are controlled by U.S. law, especially the Helium Act of 1937 which limits the sale of helium to "only such airships as operate in or between the United States and its Territories and possessions. . . ." This kept helium away from Hitler and the threatening German military.

In 1960, the U.S. government began stockpiling helium and, at a heavy cost, 42,100,000,000 cubic feet (1,250,000,000 cubic metres) of the gas has been accumulated and stored in underground wells at Amarillo, Texas. These reserves, at the present rate of consumption and without further mining, will last for the next 200 years.

This stockpiling program is today in a deep financial hole, having already paid out hundreds of millions of dollars to acquire the helium, with additional breach of contract suits totalling more than $300 million still pending against the government. In addition, it is costing the taxpayers $8 million annually just to maintain the stockpile. Without taking some positive steps toward establishing an airship industry, there is little chance that the U.S. government will ever use up this massive, costly reserve of helium, and it is restricted by law from making it available at reasonable prices abroad. The Helium Act now serves only to impede international airship development, and is especially archaic since the U.S. no longer has a monopoly on helium production.

Contours of Some Non-Rigid Airships

A. NAVY D
    (U.S.A. — 1919)

B. ARMY A—4
    (U.S.A. — 1919)

C. ARMY OB—1
    (U.S.A. — 1922)

D. ARMY TC—6
    (U.S.A. — 1924)

E. K—1
    (U.S.A. — 1931)

F. ZPG—2W
    (U.S.A. — 1955)

G. SS TWIN
    (ENGLAND — 1918)

H. WDL—1
    (GERMANY — 1972)

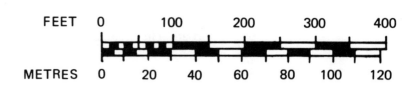

FEET	0		100		200		300		400

METRES	0	20	40	60	80	100	120

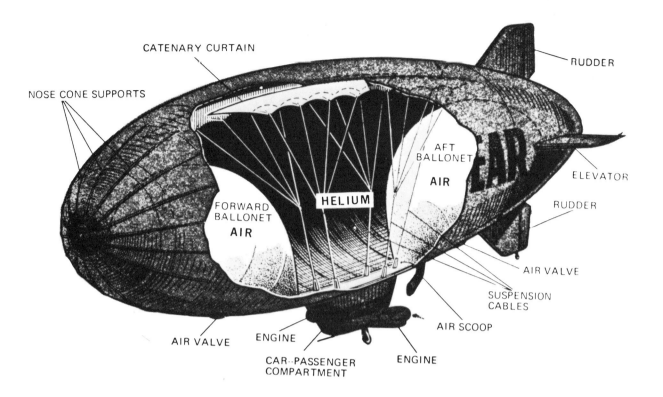

CATENARY CURTAIN

NOSE CONE SUPPORTS

RUDDER

AFT
BALLONET
AIR

ELEVATOR

RUDDER

HELIUM

FORWARD
BALLONET
AIR

AIR VALVE

SUSPENSION
CABLES

AIR VALVE

ENGINE

CAR-PASSENGER
COMPARTMENT

AIR SCOOP

ENGINE

NON-RIGID DESIGNS

The non-rigid airship, or blimp, is essentially a large, shaped fabric enclosure (envelope) with air bags (ballonets) inside. The gas bag must be kept under pressure in order to keep its shape. This is accomplished by pumping air into the ballonets through air scoops. At sea level the ballonets are full of air and trapped helium fills the remainder of the envelope. As the blimp ascends, the helium gas expands and less air is needed in the ballonets to maintain a rigid shape. The point at which the ballonets are empty and the helium fills the entire envelope is known as the pressure height. This is the maximum altitude for the non-rigid airship without allowing expensive helium to escape by valving, or releasing any extra weight (ballast) carried on board. As the blimp descends, air is pumped back into the ballonets to maintain pressure in the envelope as the helium is compressed. There is a helium valve available to make quick descent possible by releasing some of the lifting gas.

The battens at the nose cone help to maintain the shape of the envelope, and also reinforce it against the strains which occur when the ship is attached to the mooring mast. There is no rigid surface on which to attach the passenger compartment, so this weight is distributed to the envelope

The rudders (at top and bottom) and elevators (at the sides) control the direction of the blimp's flight.

(Below) The blimp, unlike an airplane, does not require large powerful engines.

The U.S. Navy's ZPG-3W, the largest non-rigid airship ever built, was over 400 feet (120 metres) long.

by the catenary curtains, a system of suspension cables which stretch from top to bottom inside the envelope and maintain the blimp shape.

The rudders and elevators perform much as they do on an airplane, providing steering and stability control. Power for manoeuvring and forward propulsion is provided by engines attached to the passenger compartment. The pilot's cabin is located in the front of the car, or gondola, and all of the control functions are performed mechanically from this post.

The volume of trapped helium determines the useful load-carrying capacity. The blimp is essentially a low-altitude aircraft since the envelope is usually a neoprene-coated dacron and this material cannot withstand the pressures which accompany flight at high altitudes.

The word "blimp" was thought for many years to have originated from a military designation for a British World War I airship known as "Balloon, Type B, Limp." Investigations later revealed that the British never had an airship designated "limp" before, during or after the war. Current opinion holds that the name originated from the odd noise emitted from the taut fabric cover when plucked.

Contours of Some Rigid Airships

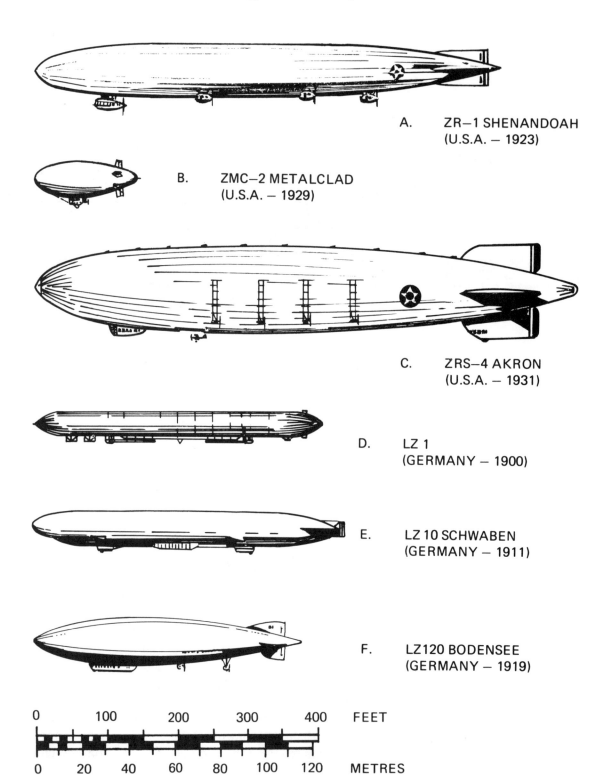

A.   ZR–1 SHENANDOAH
(U.S.A. – 1923)

B.   ZMC–2 METALCLAD
(U.S.A. – 1929)

C.   ZRS–4 AKRON
(U.S.A. – 1931)

D.   LZ 1
(GERMANY – 1900)

E.   LZ 10 SCHWABEN
(GERMANY – 1911)

F.   LZ120 BODENSEE
(GERMANY – 1919)

0   100   200   300   400   FEET

0   20   40   60   80   100   120   METRES

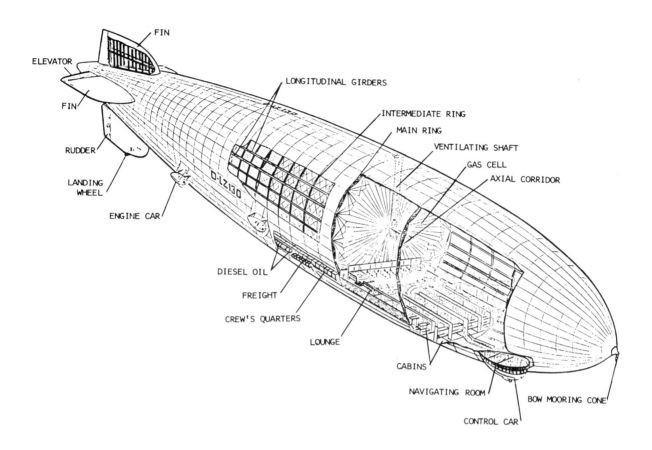

FIN

ELEVATOR

FIN

RUDDER

LANDING WHEEL

ENGINE CAR

LONGITUDINAL GIRDERS

INTERMEDIATE RING

MAIN RING

VENTILATING SHAFT

GAS CELL

AXIAL CORRIDOR

DIESEL OIL

FREIGHT

CREW'S QUARTERS

LOUNGE

CABINS

NAVIGATING ROOM

CONTROL CAR

BOW MOORING CONE

RIGID DESIGNS

The rigid airship has certain features in common with the simple blimp. The rigid has a huge envelope and gas cells, rudders and stabilizers for control and engines for propulsion. However, the rigid airship is a huge creation, and the massive size requires complex metal frameworks within the envelope to maintain its shape. The largest non-rigid in history was the U.S. Navy ZPG -3W, with a total length of 403.4 feet (122.8 metres) and a capacity of 1,516,300 cubic feet (42,900 cubic metres). Compare this to the largest rigid ever built, the *Hindenburg,* with a length of 803.8 feet (245 metres) and a capacity of 7,062,940 cubic feet (200,000 cubic metres).

The envelope of the old rigid was made of a strong fabric which was waterproofed. The large size of the airship was attained by using aluminum or duralumin girders. The framework consisted of nearly circular rings braced with wires of hard drawn steel. These were held together along the length of the ship with longitudinal girders. Between each set of transverse rings were separate gas-tight cells which filled the whole area when 100 per cent inflation was attained. For safety, even one or two cells could

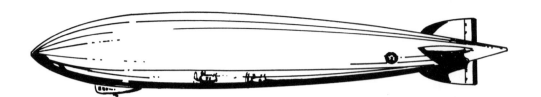

G.   LZ 126 ZR–III LOS ANGELES
     (GERMANY – 1924)

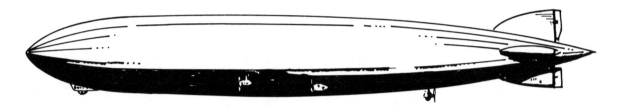

H.   LZ 127 GRAF ZEPPELIN
     (GERMANY – 1928)

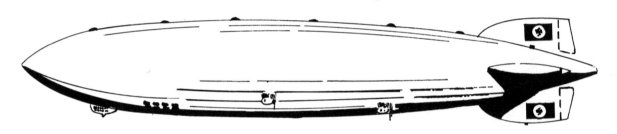

I.   LZ 129 HINDENBURG
     (GERMANY – 1935)

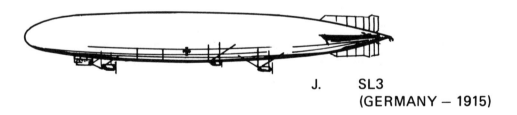

J.   SL 3
     (GERMANY – 1915)

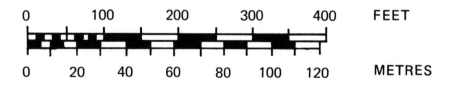

FEET

METRES

20

keep the ship airborne. The control surfaces and gondolas were attached directly to the metal framework.

The rigid airship in the 1930's was considered the epitome of luxurious travel. It virtually floated in the air and was thought of as one of history's most extraordinary and romantic creations. Millions were thrilled just by watching them and, even 40 years later, anyone who ever travelled to Europe by rigid airship retains a memory of the most enjoyable and thrilling voyage that they have ever undertaken.

K.   R9 CLASS
      (ENGLAND — 1916)

L.   R80 CLASS
      (ENGLAND — 1920)

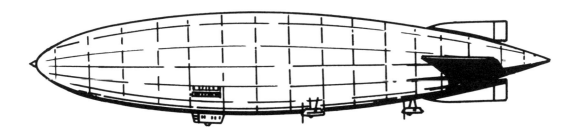

M.   R100
      (ENGLAND — 1929)

0	100	200	300	400	FEET

0	20	40	60	80	100	120	METRES

Contours of Some Semi-Rigid Airships

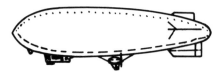

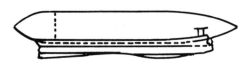

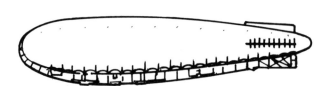

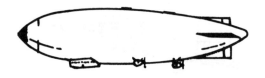

A. RS—I
(U.S. A. — 1925)

B. CB—II
(FRANCE — 1910)

C. M—IV
(GERMANY — 1914)

D. T—34, ROMA
(ITALY — 1920)
BUILT FOR U.S. ARMY

E. N—1, NORGE
(ITALY — 1926)

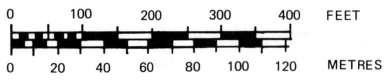

0   100   200   300   400   FEET

0   20   40   60   80   100   120   METRES

rigid keel

SEMI-RIGID DESIGNS

The semi-rigid airship incorporates a rigid keel running from nose to tail in a design otherwise similar to a non-rigid. It was thought by some that a semi-rigid airship would be lighter than a non-rigid, since it would require less inflation pressure to keep the envelope rigid. The keel structure also provided a convenient way to distribute the weight of the car to the fabric envelope, thereby eliminating the need for a complex catenary curtain. The keel structure in fact added more weight than it saved in pressurization, and is not an important part of the modern airship scene. There were, however, a number of important semi-rigid designs in the past, including the *Norge,* which made a historic flight across the North Pole with explorer Roald Amundsen in May, 1926.

The semi-rigid "Republique" was built for the French Army in 1908 by the Lebaudy brothers and Henri Julliot.

History of Airship Development

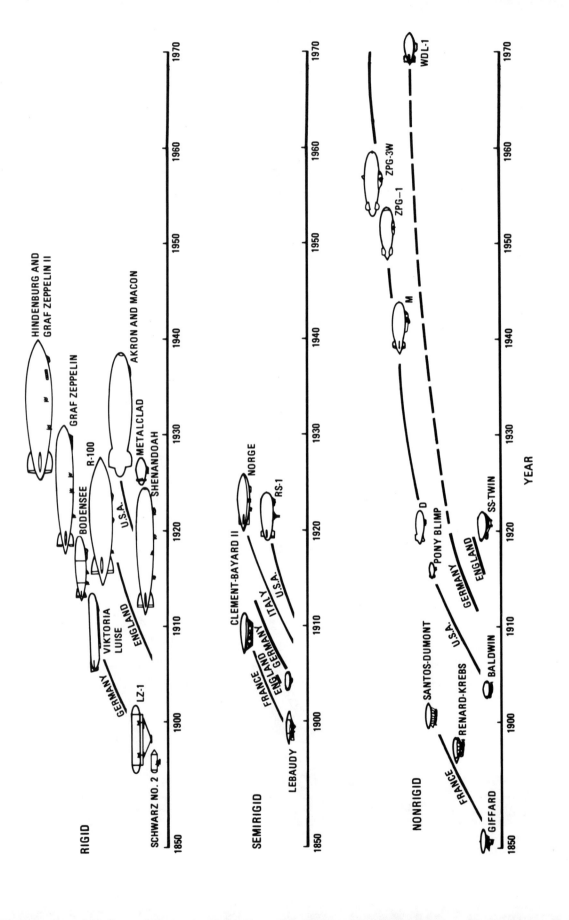

Francesco de Lana-Terzi published this design for an "aerial ship" in 1670.

the beginnings

A convenient time to pick up the history of the airship is the 13th century, when the Englishman Roger Bacon, Franciscan monk and pioneer in scientific speculation, considered the possibility of human flight with rarefied air or liquid fire. Four hundred years later, Francesco de Lana-Terzi, an Italian Jesuit priest, came forth with the idea of an "aerial ship" upheld by four thin-walled copper spheres devoid of air. Given the state of scientific knowledge in 1670 this seemed to be a practical design. He didn't imagine that the atmospheric pressure at high altitudes would have caused the spheres to collapse, or that the ship floats in the air rather than on it so that propulsion could not be attained by the use of sails or oars.

The pursuit of a practical
propulsion system for a
lighter-than-air craft
produced some strange
and fanciful designs.

These three scientific pioneers, Henry Cavendish (left), Joseph Priestly (middle) and Antoine Lavoisier (right) performed extensive research into the properties of gases, including hydrogen.

The Montgolfier Brothers

It wasn't until the second half of the 18th century that real progress towards flight in lighter-than-air craft was made. Henry Cavendish, Joseph Priestly and Antoine Lavoisier made numerous attempts at constructing balloons employing highly inflammable hydrogen. The principles involved were understood but the envelope material was missing in their day. The material had to be light but dense enough to prevent the hydrogen from escaping.

In 1776, a translation of a book by Priestly, "Experiments and Observations on Different Kinds of Air," was published in France. This book came to the attention of Joseph Montgolfier, a partner in a paper-making business at Annonay, in the valley of the Rhone. He succeeded in producing hydrogen, but his attempts to harness it in an envelope of paper and silk didn't work. Later, he tried hot-air balloons.

In 1782, he made a small silken hot-air balloon which rose quickly to the ceiling of his room when burning paper was held beneath it. He wasn't aware that air expands and becomes lighter when heated. He thought that the combustion produced some sort of buoyant gas akin to hydrogen.

With the help of his brother, Etienne, they carried out experiments in the open air with much larger balloons using a weird variety of combustible materials, but finally settling on a mixture of chopped straw and chicken dung. This mixture burned slowly and produced an abundance of evil-smelling smoke.

When the first hydrogen balloon fell to earth, frightened villagers attacked it, tearing it to ribbons.

Between 1782 and the spring of 1783, the brothers made several trial balloons and, after repeated successful flights, agreed to a public display at Annonay. On June 5, 1783, one of their balloons rose to a height of 6,000 feet (1,800 metres) and opened the era of flight to the world.

The news that two industrialists with no scientific background had successfully launched a man-made construction into the heavens so shocked the French Academy of Science that they suddenly found the money to finance a small balloon to be filled with the gas which had only recently been thoroughly studied by Cavendish—hydrogen. The first effort of the team of J. A. C. Charles and the Robert brothers produced a balloon that rose nearly 3,000 feet (900 metres) and descended near Gonesse, 15 miles (24 kilometres) away. It landed on a farm, the unlettered, half-deflated balloon descending without warning from the sky. The farmers thought it was some monstrous visitor from outer space and attacked it with pitchforks and other farm tools. Needless to say, the envelope was in shreds by the time the authorities reached the spot.

Three weeks later, the Montgolfier brothers demonstrated their invention at Versailles before Louis XVI. They had expected the balloon to rise at least 12,000 feet (3,600 metres) but because of leakage, it barely rose

(Opposite) The scene at Versailles on September 19, 1783 as the Montgolfiers demonstrate their balloon for Louis XVI.

28

The crew of the first passenger balloon and (below) the insignia they inspired. The motto is translated "Thus One Goes to the Skies."

1,750 feet (510 metres). It was shaped like a huge pear and measured 57 feet (17 metres) from top to bottom by 41 feet (12 metres) across and carried a wicker cage containing a duck, a sheep and a rooster. This was the first recorded passenger air travel and to symbolize this, the Army Lighter Than Air Corps adopted an insignia including the duck, the sheep and the rooster.

Many experiments took place during this time as the military conceived the idea of using the balloon to carry soldiers over the enemy lines or to spy on the enemy from the air. Toward the end of 1783, Jean-Baptiste Meusnier, a young engineering officer, submitted a paper on aerostatics which first proposed that the envelope of a balloon should contain a kind

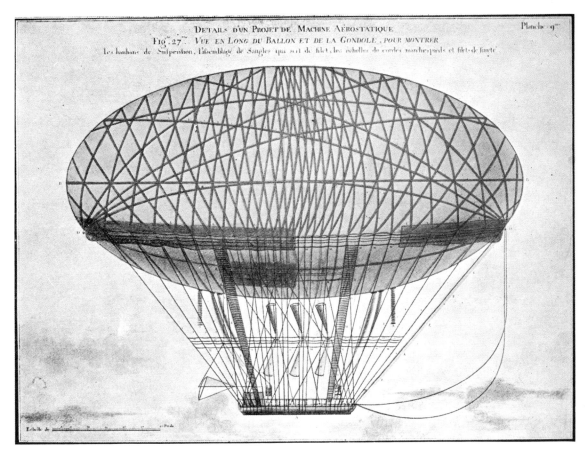

DÉTAILS D'UN PROJET DE MACHINE AÉROSTATIQUE   Planche 9

FIG.ͤ 27. VUE EN LONG DU BALLON ET DE LA GONDOLE, POUR MONTRER
Les haubans de Suspension, l'assemblage de Sangles qui sert de filet, les échelles de cordes, marchepieds et filet de sureté

Meusnier's design called for three large propellers to provide propulsion and ballonets to maintain the elongated shape.

of reservoir, or inner balloon, into which the balloonist could pump air to maintain a constant pressure inside the envelope. This he called a ballonet. The ballonet would serve as a means of conserving lifting gas and ballast in addition to playing a part in maintaining the shape of the balloon.

Henri Giffard

There were many attempts at powered and steerable balloons but the task fell finally to Henri Giffard, an engineer who specialized in steam engines. On September 24, 1852, Giffard climbed into his gondola at the Paris Hippodrome, and ordered the many men holding the ropes to let go. The dirigible gently rose and made off at a nice pace, its 3-horsepower engine hissing and leaving a trail of steam in her wake. Man had successfully made his first powered and steerable flight in a lighter-than-air vehicle—a true airship.

Thirty years later, experimenters worked to incorporate various methods of propulsion into airships similar in basic design to Giffard's. Albert and

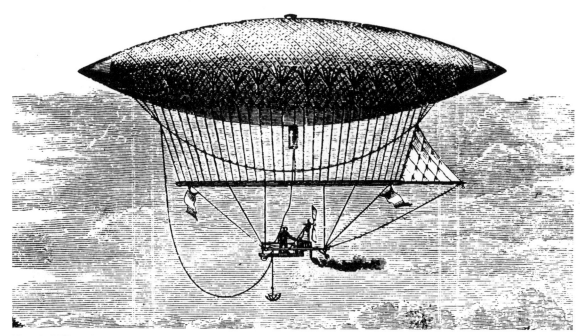

Henri Giffard's airship travelled 15½ miles (25 kilometres) on its maiden voyage, maintaining a speed of 5 miles (8 kilometres) per hour.

Gaston Tissandier employed an electric motor to propel their two-man airship, but heavy weight resulted in slow speeds and poor stability. The first airship to attain a high degree of manoeuvrability was *La France*, built in 1884 by Charles Renard and Arthur Krebs. The possibilities for directional control of lighter-than-air flight were further dramatized in the

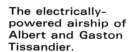

The electrically-powered airship of Albert and Gaston Tissandier.

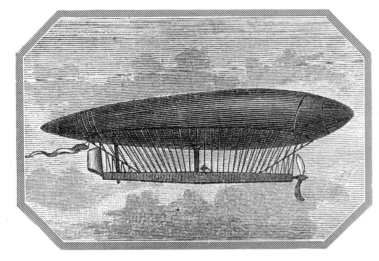

Improvements in the rudder and elevator mechanisms and lightweight equipment made "La France" the first readily steerable airship.

spectacular flights made by Alberto Santos-Dumont in his series of 14 non-rigid airships. His most dramatic flight was undoubtedly the journey of No. 6 which flew from Saint-Cloud, around the Eiffel Tower and back again, a distance of 6.8 miles (11 kilometres) in under 30 minutes. The daring flight netted him a prize of 100,000 francs and world-wide fame.

During this period the first rigid airship construction was attempted by an Austrian engineer named David Schwartz. It was a clumsy craft, made

The exploits of Santos-Dumont, a wealthy Brazilian-born air adventurer, made world-wide news. He is shown here at the beginning of his triumphant flight around the Eiffel Tower on October 9, 1901.

Santos-Dumont in his airship "No. 9" over the Bois de Boulogne, on one of his many low-flying excursions through the heart of Paris.

up of 12 rings and 16 longitudinal girders with an outer covering of sheet aluminum. The gas cells were not gas-tight, and the leaking craft fell to the ground after a 4-mile (6.436-kilometre) maiden voyage in 1897, irreparably damaged. While Schwartz's craft set no records for longevity, it did mark the beginning of the rise of German rigid airship supremacy.

A Russian airship in 1898.

There was airship activity throughout the world at the turn of the century. Shown here, the English airship "Dirigible II" in a trial ascent in 1909.

Count Ferdinand von Zeppelin

With the success of *La France* in the 1880's, the French began to consider the use of an airship for military reconnaissance missions. The accomplishments of Germany's arch-enemy caused Count von Zeppelin to sound a frantic alarm, bringing his ideas and concerns to the military

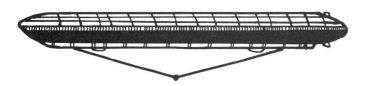

The father of the rigid airship, Count von Zeppelin, and, above, his first craft, LZ 1.

"Hansa" (LZ 13) was part of the DELAG fleet of commercial airships from 1912 until the outbreak of World War I. It completed over 500 flights.

establishment. The Count, a Prussian cavalry officer, had for many years been fascinated with the idea of using balloons for military surveillance. The new development of a steerable airship led the patriotic Count to envision a large rigid airship to be used for military purposes. He was prematurely retired in 1890 for his criticism of the Prussian war office, giving him the free time to work on his airship ideas. An electrolytic process by which aluminum could be produced in commerical quantities had been discovered in 1886, and the introduction of this light and strong metal fitted in perfectly with von Zeppelin's plans.

Von Zeppelin raised funds until, in 1899, construction began on his first rigid airship, to be called LZ 1. Built in a floating shed on Lake Constance near Friedrichshafen, LZ 1 had two passenger cars and two 14.7-horse-power gasoline engines. The maiden voyage on July 2, 1900 revealed that the power supply and the control surfaces were inadequate. The ship flew only three times.

The next four ships were equally unsuccessful, victims of poor engineering and lack of experience. It was only through the help of Kaiser Wilhelm II of Württemberg, a loyal airship supporter, and the voluntary contributions of patriotic German citizens, that von Zeppelin could continue his efforts. LZ 6 was a more successful design, and became the first ship in the DELAG company fleet. Deutsche Luftschiffahrts-Aktien-Gesellschaft (DELAG), a subsidiary of von Zeppelin's Luftschiffbau Zeppelin, operated commercial airship flights, primarily for sightseeing and intercity trips, with

LZ 7 in 1910, and continued till the outbreak of World War I in 1914. These commercial flights also served to train military crews in airship operations. The manager of DELAG, Dr. Hugo Eckener, became a renowned pilot and supporter of airship transportation.

AIRSHIPS AT WAR — WWI

The greatest strides towards new inventions and innovations are somehow tied to war and destructive ideas. The airship, like many other inventions, made its greatest strides during wartime under the Germans in their search for a better weapon.

There were four major airship manufacturers in Germany when World War I began, when all existing airships were commandeered for use in the war effort. Luftschiffbau Zeppelin, the company founded by Count von Zeppelin, completed 17 rigid airships between the summer of 1911 and the outbreak of the war. The Zeppelin Company produced a total of 88 airships for the German war effort. Schütte-Lanz Company produced a total of 18 rigids in competition with the Zeppelin Company. For some reason the Schütte-Lanz designers chose to build their structural frameworks out of wood rather than the zinc and aluminum alloy used by Zeppelin. Moisture caused the wooden frames to deteriorate, and with them the Schütte-Lanz Company. The non-rigid airships manufactured by Parseval and Siemans-Schuret found little use by the German military during the war.

It would require several volumes to chronicle fully the airship experiences of World War I. At the outset of the war, Germany alone possessed large rigid airships capable of reconnoitering or attacking distant objectives. During the course of the conflict, however, all of the major nations involved used airships in some capacity.

"Viktoria Luise" (LZ 11), also of the DELAG fleet, had a successful 32-month career.

The most dramatic military use of airships in the war were the bombing raids carried out by German rigids. The first major use of bombardment from airships came during the siege of Antwerp, Belgium, with bombs improvised from artillery shells. These bombing raids were expanded to the Russian front and, in 1915, the infamous raids on London began.

The former DELAG airship "Sachsen" (LZ 17) carried out a damaging bombing raid over Antwerp on September 2, 1914.

The airships were essentially low-altitude conveyances, but during the war, German ships crossed the border at better than 20,000 feet (6,000 metres), and could easily climb beyond the effective ceiling of any airplanes that the British or French could put in the air.

In June, 1915, both Navy and Army airships raided Britain. An airship commanded by Heinrich Mathy successfully bombed the docks at Kingston-upon-Hull using flares to illuminate the target area. About 40 homes and shops were destroyed and 64 people were killed or injured. This was the most destructive raid carried out on any English town up to that time.

Mathy's success brought demands for bigger raids on Britain, with London singled out specifically. The Kaiser sanctioned raids, stipulating that only military shipyards, arsenals, docks, military establishments and oil installations should be attacked. Precision bombing was beyond the skill of early airship crews and specific targets often went unscathed, but the raids kept up because of their disruptive effect on the British war effort and economy and the damage they did to public morale.

The German giants would silently come in the night, drop their bombs and machine gun the area, then gain altitude until they were out of range of the planes sent to bring them down. Many, however, were lost to bad weather, and many others could not climb fast enough to escape the pursuing fighter aircraft. Even though they could out-climb the aircraft, they were not pressurized and the crews suffered from intense cold and lack of oxygen at high altitudes.

The advantages of airships as offensive weapons never materialized. The German rigids proved too vulnerable in actual combat. In all about 51

A zeppelin shot down by British planes. In all, nearly half of the German zeppelin crew members in the war were lost in action.

airships were lost by the German Army and Navy, including 17 shot down by airplanes, 19 damaged by artillery and 8 destroyed in their hangars by enemy activity. Even Count von Zeppelin, before his death in 1917, realized that the airship had to be a vehicle of peace to have a viable future.

The uses of airships in a more defensive rôle were far more successful. Small non-rigid airships patrolled off-shore areas. The Navy used rigids for escorting naval vessels and for surveillance. As scouting vehicles in the famous naval battle of Jutland, airships provided essential reconnaissance information, reportedly saving the German fleet from elimination.

The Mayfly

The British Navy reacted to the pre-war German airship development with a plan to build their own rigid, the *Mayfly*. The design team, in a joint military-commercial effort, did not have the experience or the expertise to successfully imitate the Germans. After many changes in plan the *Mayfly* was finally built, but never flew. In September, 1911 the ship, inflated with hydrogen, was floated out of its docking shed when a sudden storm came up that irreparably damaged the structure. As a result of this fiasco, there were no rigid airship projects in England when the war broke out.

There were, however, small non-rigid airships available, and more were built throughout the war to aid in patrolling coastal waters. The British really entered the airship picture when their merchant vessels were under

British blimps like this one were very effective against enemy submarines.

attack from German submarines. The convoy system was introduced using airships for reconnaissance. This sharply cut the British losses and may have effectively broken the back of the German submarine supremacy of the sea.

France

The French Army attempted to operate non-rigid airships in 1917 but soon gave up their overland missions due to the heavy losses caused by enemy fire, and turned the airships over to the Navy for sea patrol duty. They achieved notable success in reconnaissance of mine fields, rescue duty and convoy escort.

Italy

The Italians have been the primary supporters of the semi-rigid construction of lighter-than-air craft. During World War I they had 10 semi-rigid airships in service, both performing naval reconnaissance and flying bombing raids over Austria.

The C-class airships were ordered for service in World War I, but were only delivered in 1918.

United States

While non-rigid airship construction had begun in the United States before World War I, the U.S. Expeditionary Forces to Europe employed French and British airships for air support while American-made airships were stationed at domestic naval bases on the east coast.

A C-class blimp before take-off. C-7 made history as the first airship in the world to fly using helium gas.

THE GLORIOUS AGE OF FLIGHT

The post-war growth of commercial airship aviation was caused by a little known episode of World War I which proved the feasibility of commerce by air. One colony of the German Empire, German East Africa, was holding out against a superior British force. The garrison desperately needed medical and other war supplies if they were to be given any chance of further defense or of fighting their way out. The decision was made by the Germans to re-supply this garrison which was 3,600 miles (5,800

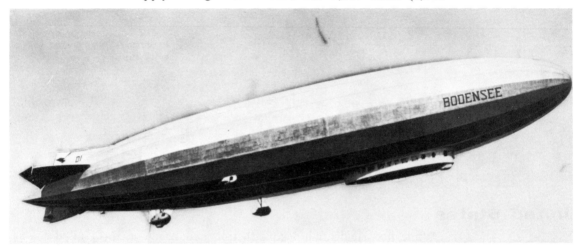

"Bodensee" served as a commercial airship after the war, with a capacity of 20 passengers plus crew.

kilometres) from the nearest airship base. It was concluded that the ship would require a still-air range of 4,350 miles (7,000 kilometres) and travelling with four engines at a speed of 40 miles (65 kilometres) per hour, be in the air 108 hours or $4\frac{1}{2}$ days. The cargo was 11 tons (10 tonnes) of small arms ammunition and 3 tons (2.7 tonnes) of medical supplies. This required a ship of 2,365,000 cubic foot (66,930 cubic metre) capacity.

On November 21, 1917, the modified L 59 took off from Jamboli, Bulgaria. It reached Africa, but was recalled by wireless before it could land, and finally landed back at Jamboli on November 25. This mission was unsuccessful only because the German garrison had already surrendered. However, the ship had carried 15 tons (13.5 tonnes) of supplies and 22 persons for a total of 4,200 miles (6,758 kilometres) in 95 hours. When they landed, the ship had enough fuel to have remained aloft for another 64 hours. This mission, which covered a distance equivalent to that between Friedrichshafen, Germany and Chicago, U.S.A., proved the intercontinental capability of large rigid airships.

LZ 126 was built by the foundering Zeppelin Company and flown to the United States in October 1924 as part of the German war reparations. Named the "Los Angeles" by the Navy, the airship was in service for 12 years and spent over 4,000 hours in the air.

LZ 126 outside the hangar in Lakehurst, New Jersey. The trip to the U.S. took 81 hours and covered 4,660 miles (7,000 kilometres).

German crewmen wanted to fly one of their ships to the United States but a complicated set of circumstances prevented it. However, it wasn't the airship but rather the bureaucracy and politics which prevented the trip.

At this time, the Zeppelin Company was on the verge of closing down; it had already been reduced to making aluminum pots and pans. However, when the United States refused to ratify the Treaty of Versailles at the end of World War I, it was an indirect blessing to the company. To put a formal end to hostilities between Germany and the United States, a separate treaty had to be negotiated. As part of the war damage compensation, the U.S. government allowed the German government to give it a rigid airship. The ship had to be capable of crossing the Atlantic Ocean from east to west. The task of building the ship fell to the Zeppelin Company which by this time was under the direction of Dr. Hugo Eckener. The ship, designated LZ 126, was finally built and safely crossed the Atlantic. The act generated considerable interest in rigid airships throughout the world and proved that even in defeat Germany remained a world power in technology.

The interest in using airships to carry passengers and mail first rose and then fell, depending on the government in power and the amount of money they were willing to spend to get the project off the ground. At first, the British had the lead in this respect; however in June, 1928 that lead was forever lost to the Germans with the construction of LZ 127, the *Graf Zeppelin*.

The framework of the "Graf Zeppelin" under construction.

The Graf Zeppelin

The *Graf Zeppelin* was christened on what would have been Count von Zeppelin's 90th birthday. On October 11, 1928, the *Graf* crew heard the command "Up Ship" as it set off on its first transoceanic voyage. The American public eagerly awaited the arrival of this historic flight, the first time paying passengers were crossing the Atlantic by air.

A sleeping cabin on the "Graf Zeppelin."

The *Graf Zeppelin* had a slim, streamlined shape. It had five 550-horsepower Maybach VL II 12-cylinder engines and could cruise at 71.5 miles (115 kilometres) per hour. LZ 127 was 774 feet (232 metres) long with a maximum diameter of 100 feet (30 metres). Its gross lift was 304,639 pounds (138,306 kilograms).

The "Graf Zeppelin" circumnavigated the globe in 20 days, 4 hours and 14 minutes in 4 non-stop stages. The engines were refueled at Tokyo, Los Angeles and Lakehurst. Only plugs and several valves were changed on the entire trip.

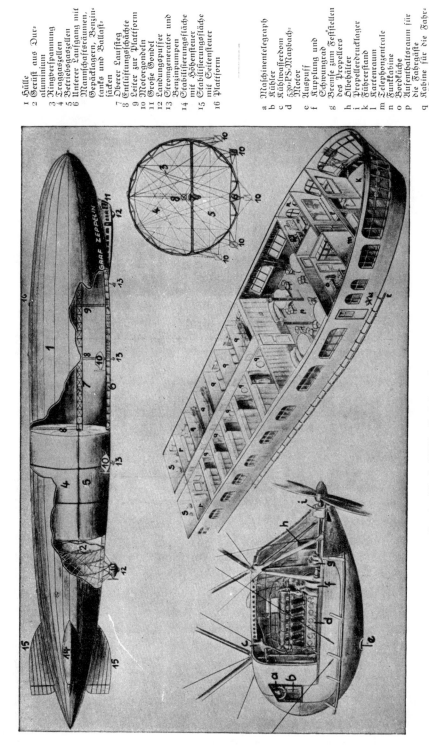

Das deutsche Luftschiff „Graf Zeppelin" (LZ 127)

1 Hülle aus Duraluminium
2 Gerüst aus Duraluminium
3 Ringverspannung
4 Traggaszellen
5 Betriebsgaszellen
6 Unterer Laufgang mit Mannschaftsräumen, Gepäcklagern, Benzintanks und Ballastsäcken
7 Oberer Laufsteg
8 Entlüftungsschächte
9 Leiter zur Plattform
10 Motorgondeln
11 Große Gondel
12 Landungspuffer
13 Stromgenerator und Benzinpumpen
14 Stabilisierungsfläche mit Höhensteuer
15 Stabilisierungsfläche mit Seitensteuer
16 Plattform

a Maschinentelegraph
b Kühler
c Kühlwasserdom
d 530-PS-Maybach-Motor
e Auspuff
f Kupplung und Schwungrad
g Bremse zum Festellen des Propellers
h Ölbehälter
i Propellerdrucklager
k Führerstand
l Kartenraum
m Telephonzentrale
n Funkkabine
o Bordküche
p Aufenthaltsraum für die Fahrgäste
q Kabine für die Fahrgäste
r Waschräume
s W.C.
t Haltestange
u Generator

Nach Originalangaben und mit Unterstützung der Luftschiffbau Zeppelin G. m. b. H. in Friedrichshafen gezeichnet von W. Goertzen
Oben: Rumpf des Luftschiffes, teilweise geöffnet. Rechts: Querschnitt durch den Rumpf.
Links unten: Maschinengondel. Rechts unten: Führer- und Fahrgastgondel.

The internal arrangement of the "Graf Zeppelin." The control room was at the front of the gondola, followed by the galley, a sitting room, 10 passenger cabins and washroom facilities. There were five 580-horsepower engines, mounted two to each side and one on the center line towards the tail.

The Hindenburg

After the *Graf Zeppelin* had completed 108 crossings of the South Atlantic and 7 crossings of the North Atlantic, plans were made to build a sister ship, the LZ 128. However, these plans were scrapped when a bigger and faster LZ 129 was proposed in 1934. Ten round-trip flights to the U.S. were planned for the first year. The new ship was dubbed the *Hindenburg* over the opposition of some who wanted to name it the *Hitler*. Plans called for inflation with 7,000,000 cubic feet (200,000 cubic metres)

The smoking room aboard the "Hindenburg," equipped with an electric cigarette lighter to minimize the risk of explosion.

of helium, but the U.S. refused to supply the warlike nation, controlled by the Nazis, with the rare gas, and the huge zeppelin was filled instead with highly flammable hydrogen.

The hull structure was 803.8 feet (245 metres) long with a diameter of 135.1 feet (41.2 metres). It was supported by miles of duralumin girders of different sizes and shapes to supply the strength necessary to withstand the stresses which the ship would be subjected to in flight under changing pressures. The *Hindenburg's* empty weight totaled 130.1 tons (118.4 tonnes). This included the hull frame, outer cover, gas cells, power plant, crew and passenger accommodations, fuel and storage, oil and ballast which totaled about 54 per cent of the gross weight, leaving 46 per cent gross weight as a payload.

There were four engine gondolas, hung in pairs in streamlined enclosures. Each housed a Daimler-Benz V-16 diesel engine. Together, they developed 1,320 horsepower for take-off and 900 horsepower for continuous cruising. The great ships required some power for take-off because of their particular type of flight manoeuvre.

The paying guests were housed in a portion of the hull. There were 25 two-berth sleeping cabins, public rooms, a massive dining room, a kitchen

The "Hindenburg" was propelled by 4 huge Daimler-Benz engines, each weighing over 4,000 pounds (8,800 kilograms).

and staff which cooked meals on board, a lounge, a writing room, wash-rooms, shower baths, a smoking room and a 100-yard-long promenade deck with panoramic windows that tilted downward for viewing the earth below. The area was divided into decks like a sea-going ship, each deck pressurized to prevent the inadvertent entrance of the highly inflammable hydrogen gas.

The great ship required a crew of 55 men, with each man assigned a specific job and many stationed 400 or 500 feet (120 or 150 metres) from the main control area. The captain was in the control section of the main cabin and had radio or sound-powered communications with each manoeuvring station. Lacking such modern innovations as sensors, transducers, transistors or computers, wherever a sensor was needed, the ship had to have a man stationed with direct contact with the captain. There were men who continually checked the pressure of the gas cells, others who monitored and controlled the ballast and ballast recovery system. It is interesting to note that the earlier ships carried sandbags which they would dump overboard when they wanted to gain altitude. The *Hindenburg* used water ballast and had a recovery system built in to recover the ballast. When the captain wanted to manoeuvre, descend or ascend, he would contact the station handling that function by internal phone.

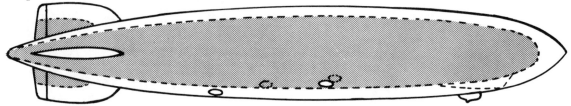

The silhouette of the "Graf Zeppelin" was more slender than the "Hindenburg" since it had to fit into a smaller hangar during construction.

The control car was a small streamlined glassed enclosure. Included inside the control room was a chart room and a room for taking drift bearings on smoke bombs which were dropped from the rear on the water. The radio room was in the keel above the control room. There was an elevatorman who sat in front of an altimeter, a variometer showing the rate of ascent or descent, an inclinometer showing the nose up or down angle of the ship and thermometers showing the gas temperature and out-side air temperature. When the captain or officer of the watch ordered, the elevatorman also handled the toggles of the manoeuvring valves in the middle of the gas cells, the ballast tanks along the keel and the emergency ballast sacks at the end of the ship. The emergency ballast consisted of four sacks each forward and aft. Each sack contained 2,200 pounds (1,000 kilograms) of water and these were used to alter the trim of the ship. The right side of the control room housed the engine telegraphs, which transmitted orders to the engine gondolas much as, in a sea-going ship, orders are relayed between the bridge and the engine room.

The "Shenandoah" was built in Philadelphia, Pennsylvania and assembled in Lakehurst, New Jersey.

The <u>Shenandoah</u>

The United States did not promote airships for commercial purposes, though from the military standpoint three great rigid airships emerged. The first rigid built in the U.S. was the naval airship ZR-1, named the *Shenandoah* ("Daughter of the Stars"). The *Shenandoah* was built following the design of the Zeppelin Company's LZ 96, which had been captured intact in France in 1917. The ship was commissioned on September 4, 1923, and enjoyed a relatively successful though brief career of 37 flights, including a round-trip transcontinental crossing. It also introduced the use of the mooring mast to secure the ship, rather than hangaring between flights. The tragic end of the *Shenandoah* came on September 3, 1925 when the ship broke in two in severe thunderstorms over southern Ohio. Even in the bad weather the ship could have survived, but the safety valves had been misused in a vain attempt to save costly helium.

The <u>Akron</u> and the <u>Macon</u>

The USS *Akron* and her sister airship, the USS *Macon,* were constructed for the Navy by the Goodyear Zeppelin Company, a partnership between the American Goodyear Tire & Rubber Company and Luftschiff bau Zeppelin which allowed the continued development of Zeppelin Company patented airships after the Inter-Allied Air Commission forbade further German Zeppelin Company operations. The two ships were each 785 feet (240 metres) long, had a top speed of 75 miles per hour (120 kilometres

53

The "Akron" had a successful 19-month career beginning on September 23, 1931.

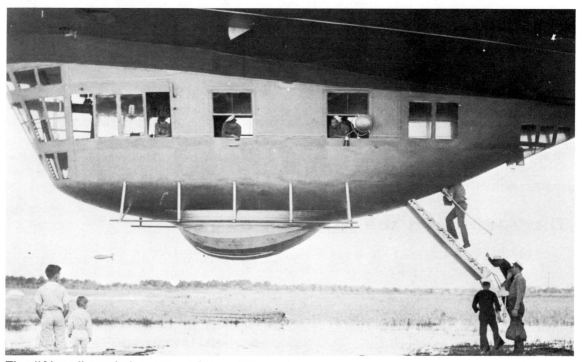

The "Akron" carried a crew of over 75 men.

The "Macon" approaches the mooring mast.

per hour) and were capable of carrying a useful load of 160,644 pounds (72,930 kilograms). They incorporated the reconnaissance capabilities of earlier airships with a new and interesting function: they served as aircraft carriers. Each had a hangar in the belly of the airship which held five high-speed Curtis F9C fighter planes. The planes were launched and retrieved in mid-air by means of a trapeze arrangement lowered through a trap door in the bottom of the hull. At one time six pilots made 104 takeoffs and hook-ons from the *Akron* in three hours. More than 3,000 such launchings and hook-ons were made from the *Macon* during her 54 flights. It is interesting to note that today, more than 40 years after the last flight of the *Macon*, the U.S. Navy has a project underway to study the feasibility of launching aircraft from an airship.

The forward compartment of the control car, USS "Macon."

Fighter planes (circled above) approach the underbelly trapeze of the "Macon."

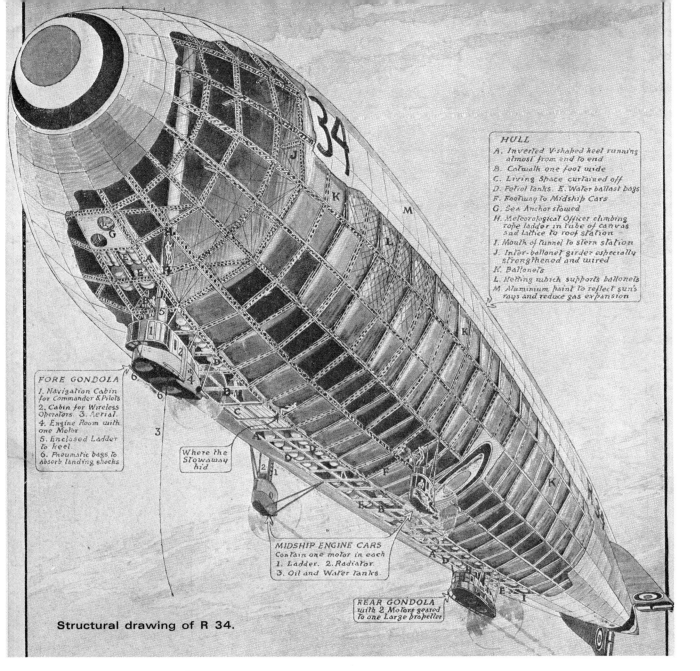

Where the Stowaway hid

Structural drawing of R 34.

British Rigids

After the failure of the British rigid *Mayfly*, there were several tentative and generally unsuccessful projects attempted. The R 29, the most interesting of these projects, was responsible for the sinking of a German submarine on September 29, 1918, when smoke bombs released from the airship marked the location of the submerged German ship for the British ships which sank it.

The R 33 class airships were by far the most successful of the British rigids, owing the basis for their design to another Zeppelin Company craft, the LZ 76. R 33 had a long (800 flight hours) and successful career, and R 34, built to the same specifications, made history by completing the first

Logbook of R 34 trans-Atlantic flight.

Time.	Barometer.	Temperature, Air.	Temperature, Gas.	Percentage, Full.	Pressure Ht. (in baro. readings).	Total change of Lift due to gas.	Change of Lift. Petrol. Tons.	Water Bal.	Various.	Total change of Lift due to ballast.	Ship's Buoyancy.	False or Latent Lift.
1.	29·70	44	42	Pressure								L ·24
2.												
3.	28·20	44	42	Press	28·70	nil						L ·24
4.	28·20	44	43	Press	28·20	nil	·45					L ·12
5.	28·20	49	48	Press	28·20			nil	nil	nil		L ·12
6.	28·20	50	49	Press	28·20		·3	nil	nil			L
7.	28·1	54	54	Press	28·1			nil	nil			L ·36
8.	28·0	57	57	Press	28·0		·31					L ·45
9.	28·70	55	57	Press	28·20	nil						L ·24
10.	28·40	67	74	Press	28·40		+ ·32					L ·84
11.	28·40	73	86	Press	28·40							L 1·56
Noon.	28·40	76	90	Press	28·40		+ ·19					L 1·68
1.	28·40	74	84	Press	28·4							L 2·84
2.	28·4	69	84	Press	28·4		+ ·15					L 2·04
3.	28·6	68	82	98	28·4							L 1·8
4.	28·3	71	80	98	28·6		+ ·2					L 1·08
5.	28·70	53	59	94·6	28·9							L ·72
6.	27·60	63½	63	Press	(27·6) 27·6		+ ·23					L 1·08
7.	27·5	69	60	Press	27·5							L 1·08
8.	27·3	57	49	Press	27·3		+ ·23					L ·96
9.	28·10	61	58	98	27·85							L ·36
10.	27·50	41	39	96	26·7½		+ ·33					L ·24
11.	27·50	47	46	95								L ·12
Mdt.	27·50	53	51	95·6			+ ·3·9					L ·24

WATER BALLAST.

Bag or Position No.	1	2	3	4	5	6	7	8	9	10	11	12	13	14	15	16	17	18	19	20	21	22
Capacity on Leaving Ground	25	25	25	25	12								25	25	25	25						
1·42					–25																	
Subsequent Alterations.																						
Final Capacity.																						

successful trans-Atlantic flight in a lighter-than-air craft. The heroic flight of R 34 came less than a month after the first trans-Atlantic flight by a plane, and eight years before Charles Lindbergh's solo achievement. It took 108 hours 12 minutes to make the 3,200-mile (5,200-kilometre) trip from East Fortune, Scotland, to Roosevelt Field, Long Island, New York. After a three day stay, R 34 completed the round trip in 75 hours 3 minutes.

H.M.A. R34 . Date July 2nd . Nature of Flight Atlantic Flight

Time	Made Good.			Thro' Air.		Wind.	Weather.	Remarks.
	Miles.	Course.	Speed.	Course.	Speed.			
1.		287.		310	40	NE 25	b	1.42 left ground. Ht 1000. all engines 1600. 1.45 Crs 310. 285
2.				various	40	NE	b	2.40 alt 240. course no reqd for proceeding down Blyth
3.					40.	NxE.	bc	4.18 q 320° 4.40 q 310.
4.	130 450	various	65		40.	NExN.	bc	6.2 q 7 q 398 to Ht q 288 Cloud height 1600. 07
5.	50	281	40	310°	38	NE 10	bc	90 Put clocks back 1 hour 9.50 stopped off engine for forward engine
6.	50	289	38	298	38	NE 10	oF.	9.55 started forward engine
7.	45	289	38	298	38	NNW 2	oF.	
8.	40	289	38	298	38	NNW	f	
9.	35	289	40	298	38	NNW 10	f.	
10.	35	289	35	298	36	NNW 10	f	
11.	36	289	35	298	35	NNW 10	f	
Noon.	30	289	35	298	35	NNW 10	f	130 reduced Walts from gar
1.	30	289	35	298	35	N 12.	f	
2.	23	299	35	320	35	N 12.	f	
3.	23	299	35	320	35	N 12	f	
4.	23	299	35	320	35	N 12	b	
5.	24	299	35	320	35	N 12	f	620 1200 ft
6.	25	299	35	320	35	NNE 12	f	6.0 Reduced height 2100
7.	30	299	35	320	35	NExE 12	f	6.50
8.	30	299	35	320	35	NExE 12	f	7.40 Std Ind bars. 16.00 Ht 3000
9.	60	299	55	320	45	NExE 12	f	8.55 800 ft. 850 1600 ft.
10.	50	299	55	320	45	NExE 12	f	9.45 forward engine stopped a repair oil pipe
11.	50	299	55	320	45	NExE 12	f	10.20 forward engine restds
Mdt.	50	299	55	320	45	NExE 12	f	16.40 stopped Port car 11.50 forward car full speed

Left Ground 44 2PM

Landed _____

Duration _____

Miles over Land _____

" " Sea _____

Details of Lift on Leaving Ground.

Petrol	35300 lbs.	15.8
Oil	2070 lbs.	.9
Water	2 lbs.	
Armament	lbs.	
Crew + gear	lbs.	4.0
Spares	5370 lbs.	.2
Drinking water	800 lbs.	.42

Total 24.32 tons

The success of these flights led to the much larger R 38, which crashed due to poor design and stopped the airship project for eight years in England.

The British airship project resurfaced in 1929 with the building of the R 100 and R 101, the first privately financed, the second a government project, but both built to the same overall specifications. As it turned out, R 100 was by far the superior construction, successfully crossing the

R 100 at the mooring mast at Cardington, England.

R 101 was not to survive its first major flight.

Atlantic twice despite some inclement weather. R 101 was the victim of government bureaucracy and the inadequate testing procedures which accompanied the hasty attempt to become airborne. The inevitable disaster occurred over France in October, 1930; the crash and fire killed most of those on board. The news was so demoralizing that the R 100 was dismantled and retired to the scrap heap, ending Great Britain's rigid airship efforts.

On the following three pages the functions of a rigid airship crew are illustrated. These drawings were made on R 101, but the basic structures and occupations are common to all rigid airship flight.

Watch-keeping Officer with Chief Steering Coxswain & Height Coxswain in the Control Car.

The Captain (& his Messenger) on the Captain's Control Bridge.

The Chef & a Steward in the Galley.

The Wireless Operator in the Wireless Telegraphy Room.

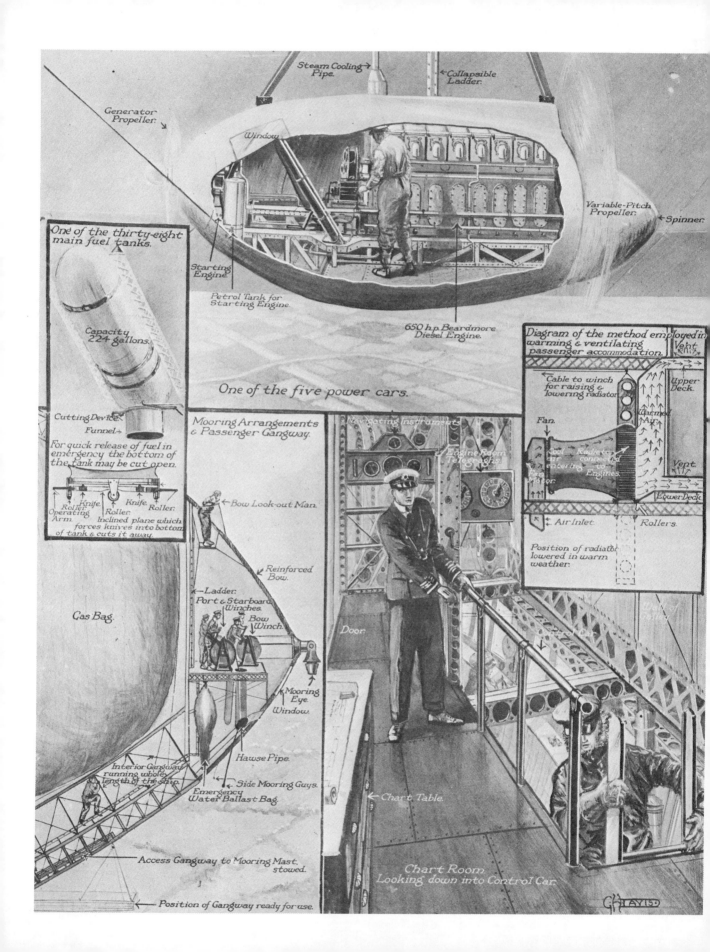

Steam Cooling Pipe.

Collapsible Ladder.

Generator Propeller.

Window

Variable-Pitch Propeller.

Spinner.

One of the thirty-eight main fuel tanks.

Capacity 224 gallons.

Starting Engine.

Petrol Tank for Starting Engine.

650 h.p. Beardmore Diesel Engine.

Cutting Device.

Funnel.

For quick release of fuel in emergency the bottom of the tank may be cut open.

Roller. Knife. Knife. Roller.
Operating Arm. Roller. Inclined plane which forces knives into bottom of tank & cuts it away.

One of the five power cars.

Diagram of the method employed in warming & ventilating passenger accommodation.

Vent.

Cable to winch for raising & lowering radiator.

Upper Deck.

Fan.

Warmed Air

Cool air entering

Radiator connected to Engines.

Vent.

Lower Deck.

Air Inlet.

Rollers.

Position of radiator lowered in warm weather.

Mooring Arrangements & Passenger Gangway.

Navigating Instruments.

Engine Room Telegraphs.

Bow Look-out Man.

Reinforced Bow.

Ladder.

Port & Starboard Winches.

Bow Winch.

Door

Gas Bag.

Mooring Eye.

Window.

Hawse Pipe.

Interior Gangway running wholly length of the ship.

Side Mooring Guys.

Emergency Water Ballast Bag.

Chart Table.

Access Gangway to Mooring Mast stowed.

Chart Room
Looking down into Control Car.

Position of Gangway ready for use.

G.H.DAVIS

A _Rigger_ examining
Under Fabric of
Hull from the
Ladder of the
Rear Power Car.

Navigating Officer "Shooting the Sun" from
the Rear Observation Post.

A _Fuel Hand_ on duty inside the Ship
attending to the Cocks on the Fuel Tanks.

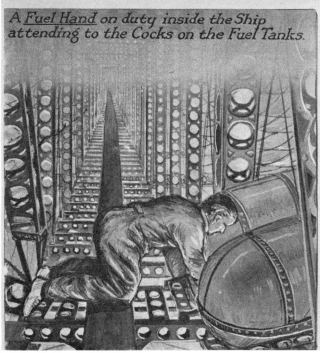

Relief Engineer going down from inside the
Ship to take his Watch in the Port Forward
Power Car.

Italian Semi-Rigids

The two most famous semi-rigid airships in history were the *Norge* and the *Italia,* both constructed by the Italian government. The first ship, the *Norge,* carried the famous Norwegian explorer Roald Amundsen and a crew of sixteen over the North Pole to Alaska. As a result of intense personal and political rivalry following the success of the *Norge* expedition, General Umberto Nobile arranged an all-Italian flight over the Pole. The *Italia* began its journey on May 4, 1928. Neither the ship nor the crew were equal to the severe weather which they encountered, and on May 25 the airship, heavy with a thick coat of ice and snow, struck the ice. Most of the crew was saved, but many lives were lost both in the actual crash and in the arctic rescue operation which followed, and Nobile returned to Italy in disgrace.

N.Y. Daily News Photo.

DEATH OF AN INDUSTRY

The "Hindenburg" left Frankfurt, Germany, Tuesday evening at 7:30 their time, and for better than 2½ days they've been speeding through the skies over miles and miles of water here to America. Now they're coming in to make a landing of the zeppelin. . . .

The *Hindenburg* had made its first ocean crossing of 1937 to South America between March 16 and 27. On May 4, she departed from Frankfurt for the first of a proposed 18 flights to the United States. There were 36 passengers and a crew of 61, with many of the crew being trained for a newer ship, the LZ 130.

Head winds delayed the zeppelin and on the evening of May 5, a new estimated time of arrival was radioed: 1800 hours on the following day. Around 1600 hours, the big ship was first seen near her destination, Lakehurst, New Jersey, but a cold front was moving east across the field accompanied by thunderstorms. Commander Charles E. Rosendahl, the station commander, advised the airship captain to delay his landing.

The arrival of the airship was not considered sensational news any longer, but a number of reporters and photographers were present in Lakehurst, New Jersey, to record the normal events associated with the arrival of a giant airship. Among these was Herbert Morrison, a reporter from Chicago radio station WLS. His live broadcast, an eyewitness account of the tragedy, gained immortality in the annals of radio broadcasting.

Well here it comes ladies and gentlemen . . . and what a great sight it is, a thrilling one. It's a marvelous sight, coming down out of the sky, pointed directly towards us and toward the mooring mast. . . .
The ship is riding majestically toward us, like some great feather, riding as though it was mighty proud of the place it's playing in the world's aviation. . . .

Around 1900 hours on May 6, the *Hindenburg* came up over the field from the southwest, at an altitude of 600 feet (180 metres), turned and came back towards the mast, heading into the light southeast wind. The engines were reversed and, as she approached the mast for a high mooring, the port and starboard yaw lines and the big mooring cable fell from the bow.

It's practically standing still now. They've dropped ropes out of the nose of the ship and they've been taken ahold of down on the field by a number of men. It's starting to rain again. The rain had flagged up a little bit. The vast motors of the ship are just holding it, just enough to keep it from . . . It burst into flame!
. . . It's crashing, terrible . . . it's burning, bursting into flames and it's falling on the mooring mast and all the folks between us. Oh this is terrible, this is one of the worst catastrophes in the world.

Four minutes after the lines touched the ground, a burst of flame suddenly blossomed atop the hull just ahead of the upper vertical fin. Almost immediately, the entire stern section was aflame, showering fragments of hot metal on the ground below, while glowing particles of fabric

(Opposite) The swastika flies over New York in this German poster advertising 2-day flights to America. Dr. Hugo Eckener, head of the Zeppelin Company, opposed the display of the swastika, but the Nazis prevailed.

whirled upward in a hot gale of flame culminating in a mushroom cloud of smoke. The stern dropped, the nose of the hull pointed towards the heavens as if pleading in prayer. Then the glowing framework broke in two, the enormous metal structure collapsed. Sixty-two of the people on board survived; 13 passengers and 22 crewmen perished.

The flames . . . oh, four or five hundred feet into the sky. It's a terrific crash, ladies and gentlemen. The smoke and the flames now, and the frame is crashing to the ground, not quite to the mooring mast . . . oh, the humanity. . . . This is the worst thing I've ever witnessed.

This was the death of the *Hindenburg,* and also the death of airship passenger service for decades to come. It has been claimed that this incident killed the airship as a vehicle for air commerce. That's not the whole story, though. It's quite possible that Hitler and Goering did more to sink the industry than the *Hindenburg* catastrophe.

It was obvious to the world that Germany led in airship technology and Hitler had been making a national symbol of the great zeppelins, squeezing every last bit of propaganda out of them. The swastika had flown over a number of American cities on the tail fin of a giant airship. The airship's potential as an implement of war would have given the Germans a great advantage, but they didn't have the non-flammable helium which they needed to avoid easy destruction. At that time helium supply was still completely controlled by the United States.

There has been continued speculation on the cause of the *Hindenburg* explosion. Some suspect sabotage; most say a charge of static electricity ignited leaking hydrogen gas. There can be no question, though, that the German political stance had kept them from acquiring the helium which would have prevented the tragedy. And in the smoking wreckage of LZ 129, public confidence in the airship died.

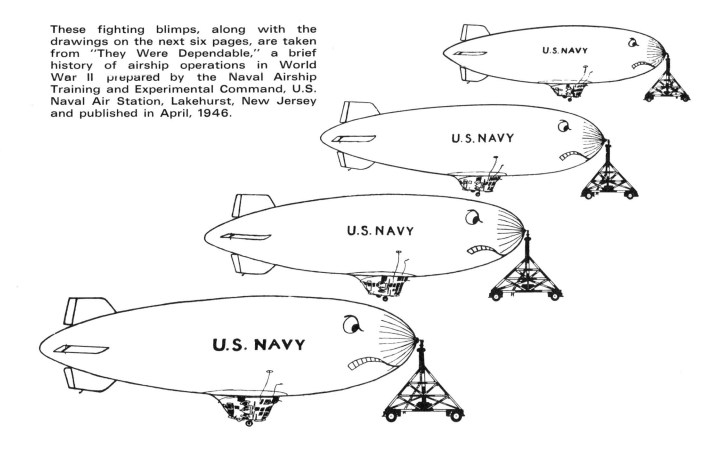

These fighting blimps, along with the drawings on the next six pages, are taken from "They Were Dependable," a brief history of airship operations in World War II prepared by the Naval Airship Training and Experimental Command, U.S. Naval Air Station, Lakehurst, New Jersey and published in April, 1946.

AIRSHIPS AT WAR—WWII

During World War II the U.S. Navy was the only service operating airships. At the time of Pearl Harbor, the Navy had in operation only six non-rigids large enough for service at sea. On December 7, 1941, Congress had approved a 10,000-plane program which included provisions for 48 non-rigid airships, but the plans for the airships were on paper only.

With the declaration of war, attacks on American shipping increased at an alarming rate, even within sight of the seacoast. The *S.S. Medio* was sunk by a Japanese submarine off California on December 20, 1941. Oil derricks north of Santa Barbara, California were attacked and generally the loss of precious ships, cargos and lives threatened the war effort. Ships were being sunk faster than they could be replaced.

The Commandants of Coastal Naval Districts recalled the success and usefulness of blimps in World War I and appealed to Washington. By June 16, 1942, the 77th Congress had authorized 200 airships, five Atlantic bases and three Pacific bases. Up until then, the only base was at Lakehurst, New Jersey and there were over 5,000 miles (8050 kilometres) of sea frontier on two oceans to be patrolled.

IN BLIMP-PATROLLED WATERS-

PHASE I

Scarcity of Airships - Many Subs - Numerous Sinkings

PHASE II

Airships Become Available - Subs Move Out - Sinkings Decrease

PHASE III

More Airships - Subs Recede Farther - Sinkings Practically Nil

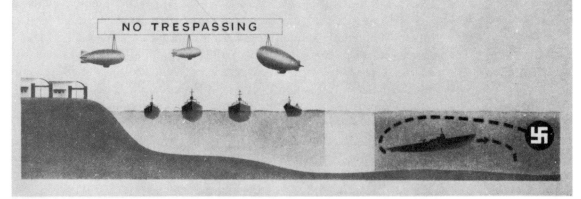

In addition to their surveillance work, the Navy blimps served to facilitate communications between ships at sea.

The airships proceeded to build up such an impressive record for protection of shipping that more airships were added to the U.S. arsenal. In the Atlantic and Gulf Coastal waters of the U.S. and in the coastal waters of the Caribbean, eastern Central America and Brazil, blimps were giving sea-going ships the necessary protection. Some 532 vessels were lost during the period of hostilities but not one single vessel was sunk by enemy submarine while under the escort of airships.

The build-up had been tremendous, from 100 pilots in 1941 to 3,000 in 1944. A large scale training regimen for pilots and crewmen was established at Lakehurst and at Moffett Field, California.

Fourteen blimp squadrons for active duty and one utility squadron were formed. At the peak of operations, they were patrolling an area of about 3,000,000 square miles (7,770,000 square kilometres) off the Atlantic, Pacific and Mediterranean coasts. They escorted 89,000 ships laden with millions of troops, billions of dollars worth of military equipment and

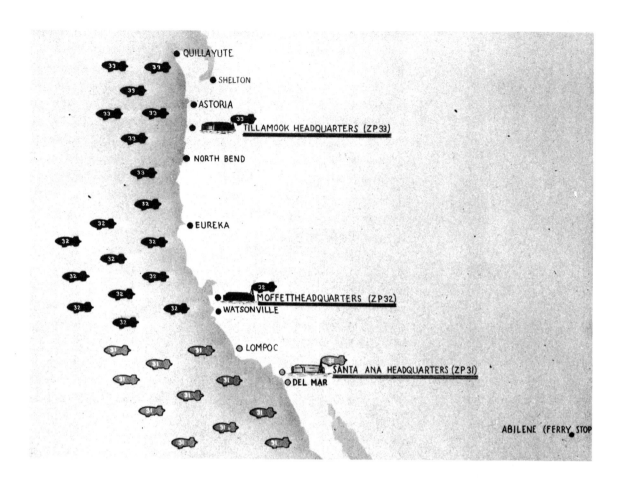

QUILLAYUTE

33 33

SHELTON

33

ASTORIA

33 33

33 TILLAMOOK HEADQUARTERS (ZP33)

33

NORTH BEND

33

32

32

EUREKA

32

32 32

32

32

32 MOFFETTHEADQUARTERS (ZP32)

32

32 WATSONVILLE

32

LOMPOC

31 31

31

31 SANTA ANA HEADQUARTERS (ZP31)

31

DEL MAR

31 31

31

31 31

31

31

ABILENE (FERRY STOP

There were a total of 14 blimp squadrons, varying in size from 4 to 15 airships each, in service during the war, including 3 squadrons on the west coast (Fleet Airship Wing Three, above) and 4 squadrons in Fleet Airship Wing One on the east coast, shown on the opposite page.

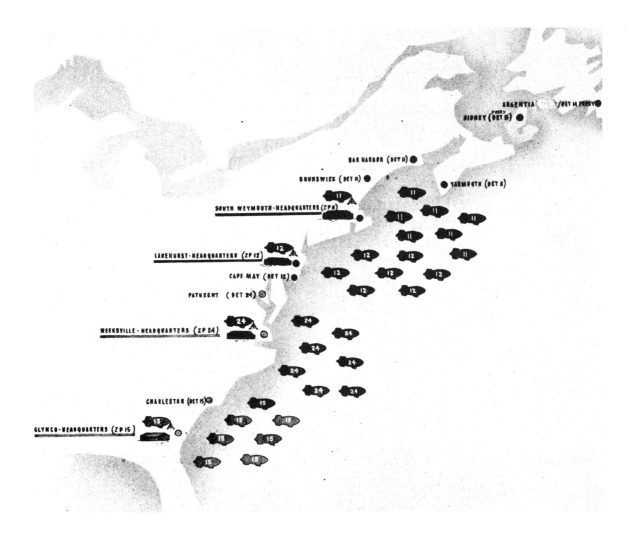

lend-lease supplies without the loss of a single vessel. In addition to their major wartime duties airships performed other useful missions, such as search operations, observations, photography, minefield clearing operations, rescue missions and assistance to sea-going vessels. The "Sick Whales" as they were nicknamed were truly dependable.

Only one airship was ever lost through enemy action. It happened on the night of July 18, 1943. In their briefing the crew had been told that no submarine, either friend or foe, was in the assigned night patrol area. Nevertheless, the ship's radar detected an enemy submarine on the surface in the Caribbean. The captain of the K-74 decided he must engage the sub in combat. This was an unheard-of manoeuvre and practically forbidden by the Navy but the airship went in with machine guns blazing to momentarily silence the submarine's gunfire. However, the ship's bombs failed to release and finally the submarine's fire brought the airship down. The ship floated for hours and all but one of her crew were rescued the next day.

Beginning in 1941 with only 10 ships, the airship force grew to include 22 L-class training ships, 8 G-class training ships, 134 K-class patrol ships and 4 M-class patrol ships.

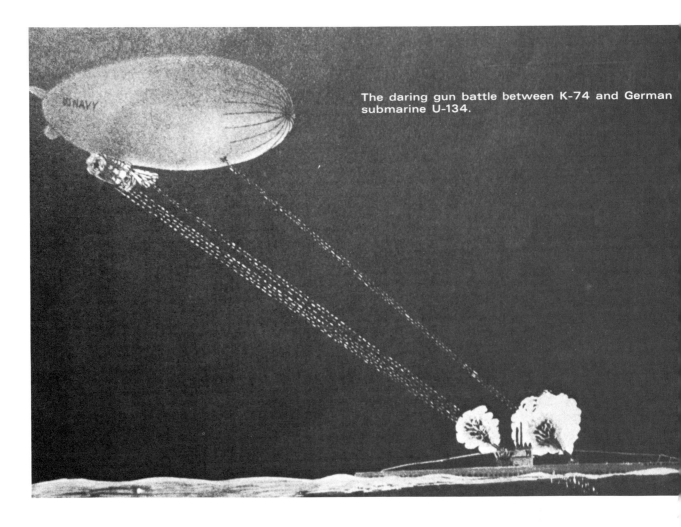

The daring gun battle between K-74 and German submarine U-134.

This incident didn't end there. In fact, it didn't end until nearly twenty years later. Since the airships had been under orders not to attack submarines when they were surfaced because it was thought that they were no match for them, the captain of K-74 lived continually under the cloud of court-martial.

It wasn't until Admiral Rosendahl (who had been the commander at Lakehurst when the *Hindenburg* burned) searched the German archives that it was found that K-74 had so damaged the submarine that it could not submerge. The submarine had finally made it to the North Sea with the help of supply ships, but was spotted and eventually sunk by British bombers.

The Navy finally in 1961 acknowledged the great feat of K-74 and wiped the tainted slate clean. The Secretary of the Navy awarded Special Letters of Commendation to every member of the K-74 crew. Lt. Nelson E. Grills, who was in command that night was presented twenty years after the event with the Navy's Distinguished Flying Cross "For Courage, Skill and Devotion to Duty in the Face of Hostile Gunfire."

The "Concorde," a prime example of the current passion for speed at the expense of the environment and economical operation.

today

THE PROBLEM WITH PLANES

The single most pressing problem in the airline industry today is the rising cost of fuel. Fuel costs account for at least one third of the total direct operating costs of a modern transport aircraft. By the year 2005, based on present usage, the U.S. air fleet alone is expected to use 769 million barrels of fuel a year. It is not necessary to present a detailed analysis of the continuing fuel crisis here. The figures are presented constantly, and it has been universally accepted that the limited supply of natural fuels is being seriously depleted. Shortage continues to drive the price of fuel upward and, with fuel prices accounting for such a massive part of the overall operating cost, the airlines are forced to raise their fares and tariffs to the public.

The price rise has directly affected passenger utilization. International passenger traffic fell in 1975, particularly over the North Atlantic route, which ironically was a major route for the rigid airships of the Thirties. Behind all of the advertising and promotional activity, the fact remains that airlines lost $84,000,000 in 1974 alone, and the trends which brought about this poor financial performance continue to predominate. Government money is funneled to the airlines through mail service contracts and even direct subsidies, but the situation remains precarious.

The airline industry relies heavily on its profits to finance future operations. New equipment must be purchased well in advance of delivery date, and the constant competition for speed and size make the new equipment essential. In fact, based on airline earnings in relation to overall aircraft economics, it is quite possible that the Douglas DC-7 and no larger plane was the overall ultimate in heavier-than-air vehicles.

The "development" in modern aircraft in recent years has been primarily an improvement in speed, and it has been estimated reliably that 90 per cent of passengers and cargo do not require this speed. Even at that, the public will often assume that the flying time is the entire time required for an airplane trip. The time spent in the air is obviously only a fraction of the travelling time, when airports have to be located far from centers of population. Often, ground travel to and from the airport takes longer on short hauls than the flight time. Travel time is further lengthened by the overcrowding of passengers and planes into limited facilities at far-out airports. Waiting in line has to be accepted patiently.

Compare travel time with the airship. Both passenger and cargo transportation on short haul trips can easily surpass airline performance and thereby become a profit-making venture. An airship needs no large airport and can, because of its low level of noise, be close to the center of a city. It can fly to more locations as it requires less complex ground facilities. It can charge lower passenger fares and lower cargo rates, which are made possible by its use of less fuel. The modern airship is a vehicle that can provide direct competition to the ailing airlines, even in total expended travel time. Whether for people or the bulkiest cargo, the airship can provide transportation at a fraction of the overall cost of other modes of travel.

STATE OF THE ART

Engineers refer to the level of technological development at a particular time as the "state of the art." While large-scale airship development stopped in the 1930's, much of the technology needed for a modern airship has been provided through developments in other fields. There are several problem areas which will require research directed specifically towards airship development. However, an airship built today, incorporating only those advances in materials, structures, propulsion and operations which already exist, would be a vastly superior craft to the airships of the past.

Materials

As the chart here will indicate, virtually every part of the structure in a rigid or non-rigid airship will profit from the improved materials available today. These new materials offer greater strength and durability along with reduced weight. They may also make possible new structural designs, taking advantage of the improved strength and weight characteristics, and may possibly cut down on the amount of hand labor required for construction.

One of the materials currently being considered for use in airships is Kevlar, an amazing new man-made fiber which is nearly five times stronger than steel, weighs 50 per cent less than nylon and requires less

Non-Rigid Airships		
1950 Materials		Today's Materials
	ENVELOPE	
Cotton/Neoprene		Kevlar/Polyurethane/Tedlar
Dacron/Neoprene		Dacron/Polyurethane/Tedlar
Rayon/Neoprene		Polyethylene Film
	CATENARY CABLES	
Stainless Steel		Kevlar Ropes
Galvanized Wire		

Rigid Airships		
1930 Materials		Today's Materials
	FRAMING	
17 SRT Alum Alloy		2024/7075 Alum Alloy
Low Carbon Steel		Titanium
Stainless Steel		Stainless Steel
		Kevlar
		Graphite
		Fiberglass
	COVERING	
Doped Cotton Fabric		Doped Dacron Fabric
17 ST Alclad		Kevlar 29 Laminates
		2024/7075 Alclad
		Fiberglass
		Sandwich Constructions
	GAS CELLS	
		Kevlar/Polyurethane
Gelatin Latex/Cotton		Polyethylene Film
Goldbeaters Skin/Cotton		Mylar Film
		Dacron/Polyurethane
	WIRING	
Piano Wire		Kevlar Ropes

The massive framework of the "Macon" under construction. Modern materials and techniques would lighten the rigid frame and decrease production time considerably.

than half the storage space of comparable nylon materials. It is non-flammable and has high puncture resistance characteristics. It is also very resistant to acids and exposure to ocean water.

So far the only major drawback to Kevlar is the rapid deterioration which occurs when the fiber is exposed to ultraviolet light. Scientists are testing different mixtures and coatings to combat this destructive effect of light. Once this problem is solved, they expect to find uses in auto tires, bullet-proof vests and dozens of other areas, including the construction of lighter-than-air vehicles.

Above, inspecting the fabric envelope of a U.S. Navy N-class non-rigid airship. Left, workmen install fittings inside the envelope. Modern fabrics can be used to make lighter and less permeable envelopes.

New materials will be used with new construction techniques to solve some of the problems of the past. For instance, modern fabrics will cut down on the permeability of the envelope, holding in the lifting gas more efficiently. In addition, there is equipment currently available which can detect tiny leaks from seams, fittings, attachments or pinholes to further reduce the loss of valuable helium.

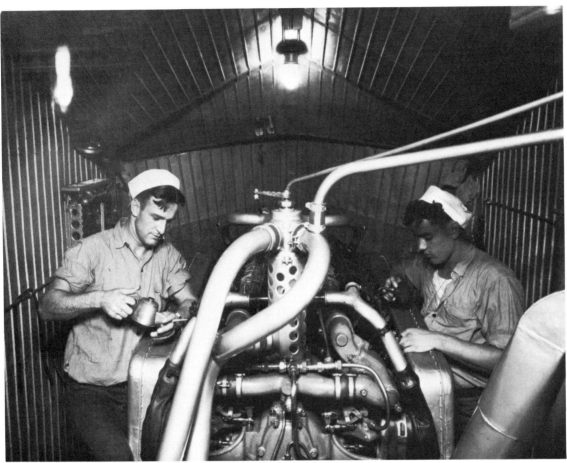

The engine room of the "Akron." Today's engines are smaller and produce more power, allowing great savings in both weight and space.

Propulsion

Some of the most dramatic advances over airships of the past will be made possible by using state-of-the-art engine technology. Today's turbo-prop engine will deliver 17 times more horsepower than a 1930 engine of the same weight. A modern engine will deliver 8 times more horsepower than a 1930 engine of the same volume. In addition, a modern propulsion system will require fewer repairs and consume less fuel than its 1930 counterpart.

Simplified instrument panel of a jet plane. Modern airships would take advantage of the sophisticated technology developed for air navigation and flight control in the past 40 years.

Control Operations

A detailed survey of the changes which have taken place in the past 40 years in the field of electronics would fill several volumes. For our purposes, we need only agree that the improvements in communications and navigational equipment will substantially aid the airship pilot in accurately controlling his craft. In 1930, communications equipment was primitive by current standards. Radio equipment required several huge vacuum tubes where today a single tiny transistor would suffice. In 1930, airship pilots relied primarily on visual sightings where, since the end of World War II, radar has been used for navigation in all commercial and military aviation.

In the 1930's, all airship control functions were transmitted by steel cables, requiring an elaborate system of tension pulleys to compensate for the changes in tension which occurred as the temperature varied. The great rigid ships required a large trained crew to handle the ship, monitoring temperatures and pressures and regulating equipment. Modern technology will provide electronic control of functions previously run by cable, and cut the crew to a small fraction of the 1930 requirement.

(Opposite) The auxiliary control station in the lower lateral fin of the "Macon." Modern control systems would make it unnecessary to station crew members in separate areas of the ship to carry out flight manoeuvres.

Handling the "Los Angeles" on the ground required a large crew in 1924–32. Today mechanical aids could cut the ground crew to a handful of men.

Ground Handling

During the age of airship aviation tremendous advances were made in ground-handling techniques. The early German rigids were docked in floating hangars on Lake Constance, and were moved in and out of the hangar by tugboats. From 1910 on, the airships relied on ground crews of several hundred men for docking and undocking. The large wartime zeppelins required as many as 600 or 700 men in the ground crew during severe weather. After each flight the airship was returned to its hangar.

The British developed the high-mast mooring system, avoiding the time-consuming and hazardous hangaring operation after each flight. By 1919 they could moor their ships with a ground crew of approximately six men. The U.S. Navy pioneered the use of a low mast and later a portable mast, similar to the current mobile mast used for the Goodyear blimps. The Navy also developed the use of ground-handling "mules," highly manoeuvrable

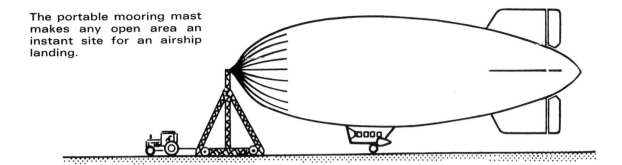

The portable mooring mast makes any open area an instant site for an airship landing.

tractors which eliminate the need for large numbers of muscular ground crewmen.

It is not expected that great changes in ground handling would be required for a modern airship. However, the exciting possibility of loading and unloading containerized cargo from an airship while still airborne has received some study in recent years. This would be especially useful in areas where there are no cleared landing areas. Substantial research would be required before such a system could be made operational, but the concept does open up some interesting possibilities.

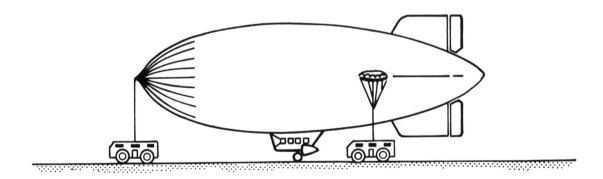

Tractors are used for holding the airship and transporting it to and from the take-off and landing site.

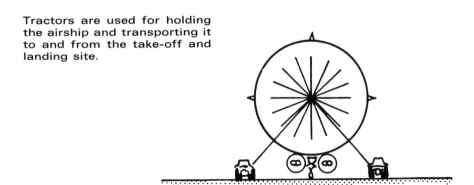

The reinforced nose of the blimp moored securely to a portable mast.

Two members of the Goodyear fleet visit the Statue of Liberty.

GOODYEAR AND THE BLIMP

Goodyear Aerospace is the unchallenged leader in the lighter-than-air industry today. Goodyear has had a long love affair with airships and it shows no sign of waning. In Goodyear territory, encompassing the Lakehurst area, Akron, Ohio, and parts of Germany and England, the idea that there will be a "second coming" of the airship is like a religion. The blimp is now considered synonymous with Goodyear. The current fleet consisting of the *America, Columbia, Mayflower* and *Europa* serve as the company's "Aerial Ambassadors" by promoting its commercial products and aiding non-profit organizations. Goodyear is proud of its airship safety record. They have carried over a million men, women and children in a half century of service without a single injury.

At times, television equipment is mounted in the blimp, and the Olympic Games, Rose Bowl football, the Grand Prix and dozens of other world sports and non-sports events are brought dramatically into millions of

The skilled crew and specialized equipment needed for blimp operations.

homes. When the 3,000 to 7,000 electric bulbs mounted on the blimp's side are lit, it is the "Super Skytacular," a flying billboard that causes untold millions to look skyward and read the message written in lights.

The blimp is a relatively simple craft, tracing its ancestry back to the balloons flown nearly 200 years ago. Each of the Goodyear ships is staffed by a crew of 23, including five pilots, 17 ground crewmen and a public relations representative. As in any other ship or airplane, the pilot-in-charge is responsible for the rest of the crew and all the equipment. He decides whether the blimp will fly.

The largest hangar in the world is the Goodyear airship hangar in Akron, Ohio, covering more than 8 acres (3 hectares).

To make the "Super Skytacular," animation is drawn with sophisticated equipment (left), then transferred to a magnetic tape which controls the bank of 7,560 lights (right).

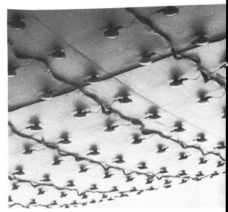

The blimp's equipment includes all the navigational equipment necessary to operate in bad weather, but since safety is a prime consideration in airship operations, it does not normally fly under adverse weather conditions. For the Goodyear ships now flying, the crews play dual rôles. They are licensed radio technicians, mechanics, riggers, electricians, lighting specialists and clerks. In addition to their regular duties, they have to handle the airship during take-offs, landings and moorings.

The crew's equipment includes a bus, a truck and a van with each vehicle and the blimp, all linked by two-way radio communication. The vehicles carry all necessary equipment, including a portable mast on the truck.

Red, blue, green and yellow lights on each side of the blimp animate "Super Skytacular" with cartoons and messages 24.5 feet (7.5 metres) high and 105 feet (30 metres) long. The lights are controlled individually or in intricate combinations through some 80 miles (128 kilometres) of electrical wiring and complex computers. A typical six-minute tape contains 40 million pieces (or bits) of information and these bits produce pictures that move in any direction.

The blimp operation can be described as a public service, since nearly 75 per cent of the messages are devoted to public service messages on behalf of non-profit charities and service organizations. The message board is made available to municipal planners, highway engineers and civic groups that need this type of vantage point to facilitate their work. The only revenue Goodyear derives from the program comes during the inactive periods at the winter bases when rides are sold.

Goodyear ingenuity has not been limited to duplicating the designs of the past. Out of Goodyear's laboratories have come such important works as the Data Link or Instant Intelligence, the Hot-Air Balloon which enables ejected pilots to be rescued in the air, and the Giant Eye ("The Eye of Heaven") which watched over Japan's Expo '70. Goodyear is involved in a continuing study of the feasibility of modern airship vehicles (MAV's) under contract with NASA.

Goodyear Aerospace has proposed that the U.S. government finance the construction of a space-age version of the ZPG-3W, the largest non-rigid airship ever built, to meet emerging needs for airborne platforms, cargo transport and military purposes. The ZPG-3W and three others like it were built for the U.S. Navy by Goodyear between 1958 and 1960.

It would be safe to say that every serious project in the world today dealing with lighter-than-air methods has a little bit of Goodyear in it somewhere.

How to Fly the Blimp

An airship pilot is a specialist who must complete a comprehensive training program and obtain his license from the Federal Aviation Administration. On the opposite page are his seat in the cabin and the controls he employs.

1. COMMUNICATION EQUIPMENT: The pilot must always maintain radio contact with the airship ground crew and, when required, with airport control towers.

2. THROTTLES AND PROPELLER PITCH CONTROLS: Throttles regulate speed of the engines. Pitch controls regulate angle at which propeller blades "bite" the air.

3. FUEL MIXTURE AND HEAT CONTROLS: These regulate the fuel-air mixture in the engine and control the temperature to prevent icing.

4. ENVELOPE PRESSURE CONTROLS: These regulate helium and air pressure inside the envelope.

5. OVERHEAD CONTROL PANEL: Contains controls for communications, fuel and electrical systems.

6. MAIN INSTRUMENT PANEL: Contains flight, navigation and engine indicator instruments.

7. RUDDER PEDALS: Regulation right and left directional control of the airship.

8. ELEVATOR WHEEL: Controls up and down direction of the airship.

91

The Heli-Stat concept (see page 142) used as a loading crane.

tomorrow

The only serious problem holding back the rebirth of the airship as an integral part of the modern transportation system is the lack of knowledge on the part of the general public. The idea of practical lighter-than-air transportation is currently being pursued by a number of individual companies, but a full-scale development program requires the commitment of money which is available only through government funding, and this money is regulated indirectly by public opinion. Everyone is acutely aware of the problems of pollution and rising prices, but few are acquainted with the possible solutions provided by LTA (lighter-than-air) vehicles. By using the equipment and procedures developed for modern airliners and space vehicles, an airship built today would be safe, economical, pollution-free and reliable.

A number of airship enthusiasts are speaking out today in government and industry. For example, J. Gordon Vaeth, director of systems engineering for the National Environmental Satellite Service, the part of the National Oceanic and Atmospheric Administration responsible for weather satellites, addressed a 1974 gathering of over 200 scientists, engineers, bankers and military leaders with the emphatic message, "The Time is Ripe for Airships." U.S. Senator Barry Goldwater of Arizona, as ranking Republican member of the Aeronautical and Space Sciences Committee, has stated that "Airships deserve a second look for the promise they hold in meeting real transportation needs." Goldwater, a former Air Force general, went on to state, in a letter to the author, that "There are no technical problems in building airships that are beyond solution."

At present, at least one major international corporation is investing heavily in the design of an airship to meet its pressing needs. The Shell Oil Corporation has contracted with Aerospace Developments Ltd. of London to design a giant airship to transport natural gas in a gaseous state. After careful study, Shell is satisfied with the economics of the airship. The Shell executives compared the proposed craft with a liquid natural gas tanker costing approximately $100,000,000 (£57,140,000) per ship and a natural gas plant costing upwards of $450,000,000 (£257,140,000).

93

When they combined the ship and the plant costs, they concluded that the airship would provide a saving of at least 30 per cent.

Several promising designs are already on the drawing boards and whole-hearted research and development could begin immediately but for one item, money, and lots of it. Up until now, the skeptics have convinced potential backers that the airship would be a losing proposition. Before discussing some of the designs presented by the enthusiasts, we should examine the skeptics' view. Remember that, in this makeshift debate, the skeptics generally represent airlines and aircraft builders, and the enthusiasts are a broad spectrum of space engineers, shipbuilders, balloonists, aerospace scientists, conservationists and environmentalists.

The 747 offers speed in transportation of passengers and goods, but the high fares keep away many travellers and make shipping of many goods uneconomical.

The skeptic produces figures to analyze a hypothetical fleet of 10 airships, each with a capacity of 40 million cubic feet (12 million cubic metres) and each capable of carrying a 500-ton (450-tonne) payload. He contends that this would cost twice as much per ton-mile as a comparable fleet of huge Boeing 747's. His figures include developing, operating costs, amortization, interest, insurance and overhead.

The enthusiasts, or "helium heads" as they have been called, have presented data before the Senate Committee on Aeronautical and Space Sciences and at a national LTA workshop, suggesting that the new airship could deliver cargo at anywhere from 1 to 20 cents (1 to 12 pence) per ton-mile. The 747 costs range between 15 and 20 cents (9 and 12 pence). The airship data was based on a vehicle capable of cruising at 200 miles (320 kilometres) per hour. However, when the speed is reduced and the cruising altitude lowered, the cost will be on the lower end of the price range. Lowered speed is a variable that the 747 could never compete with, since its cost would go up under the same conditions. Also, we should note that in the skeptics' analysis the horrendous cost of the research and development program which gave birth to the 747 was not included in the tabulations, although it was included for the airship.

94

Skeptics will also smile and state that airships are too slow, cannot buck the weather, and require a massive ground crew. This is the Goodyear blimp syndrome based on 1950's technology. Airships can be built today to travel more than 200 miles (320 kilometres) per hour, and with the new materials currently available, weather would not annoy the airship crewmen. It doesn't even bother the present Goodyear crewmen, although like any other airmen, only the foolhardy deliberately fly into bad weather. The airship would use the same sophisticated electronics to avoid the weather that is used by heavier-than-air vehicles.

Some also state that the airship is dangerous. This opinion is based not on facts or figures but rather a gut reaction to the rare but sensational failures of the past. When the figures are analyzed it becomes clear that during the period of airship aviation the number of flight hours between fatalities was actually better than airplanes in the same era and time span.

The technological problems of yesterday have been largely resolved already; the remainder can be easily solved using modern scientific methods. Changing the ideas, opinions and prejudices which have been festering for years appears to be the most formidable obstacle to the airship's revival. The original development will require the collective efforts of industry, governments and the universities. Except for Russia, which is reportedly financing a priority airship project, the other governments have succumbed to the aircraft industry spokesmen and dismissed the subject. Many airship enthusiasts claim that the aircraft manufacturer's propagandists killed the U.S. Navy's airship operations under the guise of an economy measure. Considering the extensive list of potential uses by the Navy and the impressive record of naval airships in both world wars, it is certainly suspicious that all naval airship operations were abruptly halted in June of 1961.

The development of the airship to fulfill its potential will require a lot of money. Governments and huge corporations have not been willing to invest the necessary funds. There are, however, a number of individuals and small companies proceeding, with limited funds, to carry out the research necessary to design a modern airship capable of meeting modern commercial and military needs.

WHAT CAN THEY DO?

The airship of tomorrow will have untold uses. Feasibility studies have been conducted under contract for NASA by major aerospace companies. These studies show conclusively that there are transportation markets for which the airship is the only vehicle to do the job, and others where the airship could be better, faster and cheaper than conventional aircraft. The mission analysis conducted for NASA of Modern Airship Vehicles (MAV) suggests that the following uses would be appropriate for further consideration.

Commercial Field

Scheduled Short-Haul Passenger Service
Unscheduled Long-Distance Passenger Service
Urban Rapid Transit Systems
Heavy and Outsize Indivisible Load Carriers
Platform Missions (Scientific)
Agricultural Applications
Crop Harvesting and Spraying
Chemical Seeding
Livestock Transfer
Pipe and Powerline Patrol and Construction
Aerial Survey
Sightseeing and Pleasure Cruises
Seismographic Survey over Water
Border Patrol
Air Pollution Monitoring

Water Resource Monitoring
Crop Surveillance
Fish Monitoring
Ore/Petroleum/Gas Carrier Service from
  Remote Regions
Transport of Bulk Perishable Goods
Police Surveillance
Disaster Relief Hospital
Nuclear Fuel and Waste Transport System
Nuclear Plant Construction
Geodetic Surveying
Prospecting
Traffic Control
Television Station

Military Missions

Navy
Logistics over the Shore
Sea Control
Long Endurance Shore-Based Patrol
Heavy Lift Logistics Support
Airborne Command and Control
Arctic Operations
NOAA Support (Meteorology, Aerology)
Minesweeping
Ocean Escort
Modern Airship Vehicle Flight Training
Demonstration Platform
Anti-Submarine Warfare
Missile Launcher

Army
Small Observation/Command Control
Artillery Movement System
Surveillance Drone
Unmanned Logistics Support Systems
Large Indivisible Payload Lifter
Main Battle Tank/Combat Engineer
  Vehicle Payload Lifter

Air Force
Base-to-Base Transporter
Intratheater Transporter
Remote Station Support Transporter
Time of Arrival/Distance Measuring
  Equipment Station
Remotely Piloted Vehicle Carrier/
  Launch/Control Platform
Mobile ICBM Transporter
Mobile Missile Launcher

Coast Guard
Search and Rescue
Enforcement of Laws and Treaties
Small Drone Missions
Aids to Navigation
Marine and Environmental Protection

Common Missions
Communications
Rescue and Recovery
Missile Launcher
Surveillance

Each of these missions was thoroughly analyzed using the most reliable data currently available. The market opportunities and relative value of missions were evaluated. The research and development costs were subjected to computer analysis, along with the costs of fuel and lifting gas, building materials, labor, ground handling and maintenance and much more, all based on experience from past airships, estimated costs of modern technology and the state of today's economy. The results of these studies prove that the MAV (Modern Airship Vehicles) can be built to be safe, fast enough for practical use, and profitable in commercial applications.

The military applications which have been proposed were not studied on the basis of profit, but rather of practical applicability to offensive and defensive situations. It is in the military category that the greatest hope for future financing may be found. As in many other industries, the aircraft industry most notably, developments made for military vehicles are later incorporated in commercial aviation. It is likely that, once the MAV exists in any form, commercial applications will be planned to fit the capabilities of that existing vehicle, with moderate modifications. The same vehicle which would be capable of lifting large numbers of troops could carry huge quantities of produce or industrial goods at the same very low cost. A lighter-than-air surveillance vehicle used for military reconnaissance duty could be adapted easily to police or private security operations. Traditionally, the armed services have been the breeding ground of technological advancement, since there is no expectation of an immediate profit realization and the costs of research and development are spread out over the entire tax base.

The NASA feasibility studies which have been completed to date indicate a bright future for airships, particularly for the HLA (Heavy Lift Airship), a combination of four helicopters joined to a huge helium-filled lifting body, described in detail on pages 108 and 143. The conclusions reached so far can be summed up as follows:

1. A major deficiency in current air transportation systems is the short-distance hauling of heavy and very heavy outsized cargo. For military and commercial applications, the heavy-lift airship using four helicopters was found to be uniquely suited for these missions.

2. Non-rigids are generally preferred for small sizes, metalclads for mid-sizes and rigids for large sizes. However, if Kevlar (*see page 78*) is developed as an envelope material, non-rigid construction will be superior for all sizes.

3. The heavy-lift airship concept offers a substantial increase in vertical lift capability over existing systems and is projected to have lower total operating costs.

4. VTOL (Vertical Take-Off and Landing) airships appear to be economically competitive with other aircraft and can attain lower noise levels.

5. There is a considerable foreign civil market in the off-loading of

cargo from sea-going ships in developing nations lacking deep-water ports.

6. The classical helicopter problems of high fuel consumption and airframe weight are implicitly minimized in HLA (Heavy Lift Airships).

7. The collective payload capability of four helicopters at the same range would be about 50 per cent of that for the HLA.

8. The total operating costs on a payload ton-mile basis is substantially reduced over current large helicopter vertical lift costs.

9. The HLA is competitive in fuel economy, since its fuel consumption is 30 per cent better than heavy lift helicopters.

10. The HLA is sufficiently controllable to perform the military and civil missions for which it is being considered over an acceptable range of atmospheric conditions.

11. Fabrics using existing advanced materials will give significant component weight reductions and add structural strength to combat adverse weather.

12. As to weather, no vehicle is truly an all-weather vehicle. However, many vehicles can survive and resume operations. The modern airship is such a vehicle.

13. Ground handling can be accomplished in virtually all weather conditions.

14. As to military vulnerability, the airship is capable of a credible self-defence capability. In fact, it is much more survivable than a C-5A against missile attack.

15. The fully buoyant airship concept can provide an airborne platform with long endurance that will satisfy many navy requirements.

16. An airport feeder vehicle for commercial operation could cruise at 130 knots, have a fuel cost of $.25 per gallon per ton mile and passenger costs would be $.05 per mile.

17. There are 15 airship hangars remaining in the United States that could accommodate two such HLA vehicles.

18. No major unresolvable technological problems can be foreseen for the HLA concept.

19. A flight research vehicle would be highly desirable and should be developed soon.

SAFETY

While in the public eye, safety is still an important consideration in judging the future of the airship, most experts have stopped discussing this problem. This will be more understandable after examining the following chart, which outlines the causes of the major airship disasters of history.

Fatal Accidents in Airship History

AIRSHIP	DATE	FATALITIES	% OF PEOPLE LOST	CAUSE
LZ 14	1913	14	70	Crew members drowned when ship broke up in poor weather due to poor construction design and flight procedure errors.
LZ 18	1913	28	100	Hydrogen fire caused by poor design which allowed flammable gas into engine compartment.
R 38	1921	44	90	Poor structural design caused ship to break in half.
Roma	1922	34	75	Failure of mechanical control system caused collision with high tension cable, igniting hydrogen. (MAV would not use mechanical control cables.)
Dixmude	1923	50	100	Lost in surprise storm, probably flammable hydrogen gas exploded by lightning bolt.
Shenandoah	1925	14	33	Safety valves had been closed to save helium, making proper manoeuvres in squall impossible.
Italia	1928	8	50	Poor flight command decisions in arctic conditions caused crash.
R 101	1931	48	89	Political considerations caused flight before ship was airworthy. Design flaws went uncorrected in rush to completion.
Akron	1933	73	96	Came down at sea during bad weather; incorrect altimeter reading reported. Many fatalities due to lack of lifesaving equipment on board.
Macon	1935	2	3	Structural failure resulting from inadequate repair of known damage.
Hindenburg	1937	35	36	Probably static electricity ignited leaking hydrogen; possibly sabotage. Destruction definitely caused by explosive hydrogen gas.

Two major factors were involved in these disasters. The first was the use of hydrogen as a lifting gas, the result of political considerations rather than technological failure. An airship built today would undoubtedly have access to non-flammable helium, and so one source of trouble is eliminated.

The problem of human error during flight procedures has been largely eliminated by the improved navigation equipment which has been developed for commercial aviation during the last 40 years. The techniques for ground handling have also been subject to vast improvement, effectively eliminating damage to airships before and after flights.

In the area of structural strength, the development of new, strong and lightweight materials eliminates much of the weakness found in earlier craft. The techniques of computer design analysis, in which accurate engineering decisions are made on the basis of computer analysis of stress and strength, are light-years ahead of the techniques available 40 years ago. The popular tendency to think of a modern airship vehicle in terms of 1930's technology is a serious roadblock to further development.

Airships also incorporate several positive safety features. Their low landing speed leads to a much safer landing than heavier-than-air vehicles can accomplish. The multiple engines of the airship permit normal landings in the event of engine failure. Actually, the LTA vehicle is capable of a safe landing without power under most conditions. Even if all of the engines were to fail at once, the ship could remain airborne almost indefinitely, allowing sufficient time to initiate emergency procedures. If the engines on an airplane die, there is little time for correcting the problem.

Essentially all airships are provided with emergency deballast capability, the ability to quickly drop substantial excess weight if a loss of lift occurs. The lifting capability of the airship is safeguarded by using gas compartmentalization. Dividing the ship into individual, independently gas-tight cells ensures that, even if a single cell is deflated, there will still be enough lift to remain airborne.

The safety record of the airship throughout history is extremely respectable. Figures prepared by the Durand Committee, set up in 1936 by Presidential authority to study airship operations, show that the safety record for airships was consistently as satisfactory as, if not better than, the record for airplanes. The experience of the Goodyear Company, the only major LTA manufacturer in recent years, is very impressive. After 45 years of commercial operations, carrying over a million men, women, and children, there hasn't been one scratch or bruise. The airships are equipped with the latest navigational and safety devices, comparable to those found in a modern jetliner, and all are approved and licensed by the Federal Aviation Administration.

The major consideration holding back the rebirth of the airship is clearly not safety, but profit.

The "Akron" over Washington, D.C. Airships can fly over the heart of a city without disturbing the businesses and homes beneath.

THE ADVANTAGES

Airships vs. Pollution

Every day millions of cars, trucks, trains and planes pour their poisonous exhaust fumes into the air we breathe. Scientists continue to attempt treatment of these fumes to render them harmless, but the processes they have found are too complex and costly to be practical. The simplest way to cut down on air pollution is to cut down on the amount of fuel we burn, and there is no form of overland transportation which can compete with the airship in fuel economy.

The immense weight of trucks and trains requires great quantities of fuel just to move the vehicle itself, without even considering the weight of the cargo. The airship is virtually weightless in the air, requiring smaller engines and lower fuel consumption for propulsion. In addition to the fuel saved through the airship's natural lightness, there is the additional savings made possible by a direct aerial route, as opposed to the winding highways and railways needed for surface transportation.

The natural forces which keep an airship aloft provide a great advantage over the airplane in fuel consumption. An airplane must create lift by hurtling through the air at high speeds, speeds which do not allow efficient fuel use. A substantial portion of the fuel consumed in an airplane flight goes to provide the lift needed to reach cruising altitude. The airship floats upward, saving fuel and cutting down the amount of poisonous engine exhaust we will have to breathe.

The other form of pollution, noise pollution, has only recently become widely recognized, but scientists warn us that the noise level in today's environment, particularly in regions of heavy air traffic, causes both physical and psychological damage in humans. In this area the airship clearly has no rival. The airship passes overhead silently, gliding by without the roar of airplanes, trucks or trains. Even in landing, the noise made by a modern airship would not cause the surrounding population the hardships imposed by today's airports. If plans can be developed for unloading an airship without landing, the silence will be complete, and certainly welcome.

These bananas are being harvested in Guatemala. Air transport would be too expensive for this lightweight bulky crop, so the bananas will be chemically treated for preservation and sent by truck, rail and ship to their destination. Airships could pick up the produce at its source and deliver it quickly and directly to the market.

Low-Density Cargo

Conventional aircraft are designed to carry cargo which is compact and fairly heavy. The shipping problem is generally one of finding room to put the freight, rather than compensating for the weight of the object to be shipped. The larger the plane the more expensive it is to operate and the more difficult it is to fly safely. In addition it requires more complex and expensive ground facilities.

The opposite effect holds in the design of an airship. If an airship is built larger, the volume of gas contained in the envelope grows faster than the area of the envelope needed to contain it, following the square-cube

The size of a cargo plane determines the practical payload, rather than the weight of the goods to be transported.

law (see glossary). The weight of the airship does not increase as quickly as the lift as the size increases. In addition, a larger airship does not require a proportionately larger crew. Thus, a giant airship which can hold great quantities of lightweight freight is an economical concept.

The airship's ability to carry low-density, bulky cargo will be especially useful in the transportation of produce and other perishable foodstuffs. At present, farmers find that railroad schedules are too slow, with delays sometimes resulting in perishables spoiling before they can reach the marketplace. Trucks are also unpredictable in terms of speed and reliability, and more expensive than trains. Regular air freight charges for lightweight goods like lettuce or shellfish are more than the goods themselves are worth.

Many farmers and fishermen would welcome an airship transportation system which would allow them to offer their goods at competitive prices around the country and even around the world. They cannot, however, finance a program of airship development by themselves. If the funds for development are found and a working airship vehicle is built, the volume of low-density cargo would provide a large influx of profit-making shipping business for the airship operator.

This oil drilling site in the Guatemalan jungle could be built only after an airstrip was painstakingly carved in the undeveloped countryside. Airships could deliver drilling equipment to remote areas more economically, without elaborate terminal facilities.

Oversize Payloads

There are virtually no restrictions on the size of an airship, since the larger it is, the more lifting gas it can contain. Once again, the airship resembles the ocean-going ship in its ability to serve as a barge to transport massive objects. However, the airship can go anywhere, while the ship is limited to the seas and large inland waterways.

Consider the growing number of nuclear power plants needed to meet expanding energy requirements. A nuclear power plant requires certain large components weighing between 50 and 400 tons (45 to 360 tonnes), components which must be shipped in whole units. In the past they have been moved on barges, requiring a shorefront construction site. Companies are currently involved in studying the technology required to move these huge components with the tremendous lifting power of airships.

There are other large manufactured goods currently available which would benefit from airship transportation. Houses, for instance, could be entirely prefabricated at the factory and flown into position, providing tremendous savings in on-site construction costs. The savings made possible by shipping entire constructions which have been put together in an economical mass production system rather than shipped piece-by-piece to a construction site and assembled by individual groups of workers would justify the research and development of modern airships, even if there were no other practical uses. However, manufacturers cannot change their production system until they know that the required new technology exists to justify the change. Once the airship has been proven a reliable means of transportation, industry will employ this new tool to save money and improve productivity in hundreds of ways. However, the specialized companies which would use an airship transportation system cannot afford to develop the system themselves. Once again, we see the need for government development funds. The resulting technology will provide a substantial boost to national industrial development.

Three blimps can be moored in a small space without an expensive ground handling set-up.

Terminal Facilities

The airship would not require the complex system of runways and hangars needed by aircraft today. A totally buoyant airship could lift straight up, eliminating the need for long runways. While the home base of the airship would probably require the same kind of support technology required by today's aircraft, the airship can stop at intermediate points without complicated facilities. The techniques of ground handling have advanced to the point where only a few men and a portable mooring mast are required for safe and speedy arrival and departure.

The MAV would enable us to move goods and equipment where the only access in the past has been on foot or dirt road. Where no roads or airfields now exist, the use of airships would enable us to make use of the tremendous untapped resources of the earth. In this way, the airship will not only save our natural resources, but open up new sources of valuable fuel and other materials.

Ships are an inexpensive means of transportation, but time and money is lost in switching cargo to an inland conveyance.

Convenience

The airship can go anywhere, over land or sea, which provides a great saving of both time and money over today's commercial transport system. A great deal of time is lost moving cargo from one form of transportation to another. For instance, cargo moved by air freight must then be moved by truck from the airport to its destination, and airports are few in number and far from centers of population. A ship can transport many types of freight with great economy, but can only travel by water, and cargo must be transferred to surface transportation systems for the trip inland. If trains are employed, the freight cars must wait until there is a sufficient number of cars for a particular destination, and even at that destination the goods must again be transferred to trucks for delivery. Many kinds of produce today are shipped by truck to a train to a ship to another train to another truck to the destination. The airship can avoid these handling problems by providing the capabilities for land and sea travel of commercial airplanes, without imposing the tremendous price of air freight.

Running water aboard the "Akron." The size of the airship allows comfortable accommodations for the crew on extended missions.

Long Endurance Flights

The airship does not require fuel to stay aloft. This basic fact, central to most of the applications foreseen for the MAV, enables the establishment of stations in the sky capable of moving where they are needed and remaining always aloft and ready to respond to emergencies. The airship has been used as a surveillance vehicle in military situations in both world wars. Brought up to date, the airship can provide a platform in the sky for observing military movements or criminal activities.

It has been suggested that a giant airship which is within the capabilities of current technology could serve as a flying hospital, bringing the finest medical facilities to disaster victims with unprecedented speed. Helicopters which are currently used for disaster relief can bring in the proper medical personnel, but cannot fly in the equipment used in modern hospitals. Helicopters are expensive to operate, and cannot compete with the lifting capability of the MAV.

Low fuel consumption allows extended flights without refueling, giving the airship an exceptional non-stop flight range.

Goodyear Aerospace, in a study undertaken for NASA, has recommended the combined helicopter-airship heavy lifter as an economical commercial vehicle and military transport. The technology is readily available for construction of a test vehicle.

THE ECONOMICS OF MODERN AIRSHIPS

Any new method of transportation must offer an improvement over existing systems in terms of performance and cost, or must be able to perform missions which no others can accomplish and still return a profit. To attract investors, the airship must capture traffic from other modes of transportation. Airship designers and experts in the aeronautics field have made preliminary attempts to project the costs associated with producing a modern airship. There are certain basic costs which can be estimated with a high degree of accuracy at this time, including:

- Salaries for crew and company personnel
- Base development and running cost
- Fuel
- Helium
- Auxiliary transport
- Maintenance
- Miscellaneous administrative costs

Other costs have been estimated, relying on the history of past airships and experience in related technological projects. These costs include:

- Research and development costs
- Building costs
- Insurance costs

On this basis, several studies have been made to prove or disprove the economic practicality of airships. It is a confusing mass of data, and it must be admitted from the start that this side of the airship picture is more cloudy than the technological side. Virtually everyone involved in the field agrees that the technology to build modern airships exists today, and the problems which remain could be solved in a short time using accepted research procedures and techniques. The problem, then, is trying to nail down the value of such a project. It must be stressed that military applications are numerous, practical, and tremendously important to the continued advancement of the LTA field. Relative values of military projects in money terms are often difficult to comprehend, however, as they rely to some extent on tactical decisions beyond the understanding of most civilians. We can, however, consider the economics of commercial LTA aviation.

Numerous comparisons support the projected MAV. For instance, an airship with a capacity of 22,000,000 cubic feet (660,000 cubic metres), that is, three times the size of the *Hindenburg*, with conventional propulsion and conservative design, could carry a payload of 655,000 pounds (295,000 kilograms) for a range of 2,950 miles (4,720 kilometres) and 326,000 pounds (146,000 kilograms) for a range of 6,500 miles (10,500 kilometres). With nuclear power, the 655,000-pound payload would remain the same regardless of the range. In comparison, the C-5A is considered to be the largest cargo aircraft practical. The C-5A could carry only 265,000 pounds (120,000 kilograms) for 2,950 miles (4,750 kilometres) and only 80,000 pounds (36,320 kilograms) for 6,500 miles (10,500 kilometres). In addition, the C-5A requires special runway facilities which would be expensive to construct.

Another comparison bears noting; an estimate of the cost of the Alaskan Pipeline exceeds $6,000,000,000 (£3,430,000,000)—that is with the expectation of piping a capacity of 2,000,000 barrels a day to one point within five years after it begins operating. Initially, it is only expected to have a capacity of 600,000 barrels per day. Even here, the airship's overall estimates are much better. A fleet of 115 vehicles would cost $3,875,000,000 and could transport 1,000,000 barrels per day, discharging the oil at various locations around the country. Experts now foresee storage problems resulting from the quantity of oil arriving by pipeline at one location in a short period of time.

Any data which present specific performance figures for a vehicle that does not exist yet must be regarded with suspicion. In the charts which follow, prepared for the U.S. Senate hearings of July 1974, the trends which were evident from the available data are indicated without hard figures. They are presented here to provide an idea of the effect of speed and size requirements and the number of airships to be produced on the cost of the MAV.

If we make only range-endurance and fuel economy the dominant factors, it can be easily shown that the MAV offers performance and capability far better than competing systems.

The one single factor besides labor costs which is driving air freight rates out of sight is the rapidly climbing cost of fuel.

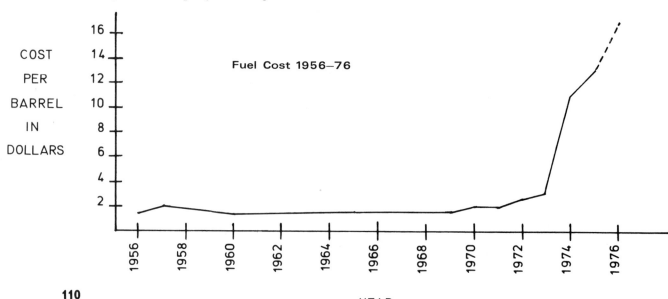

The airship would use a fraction of the fuel now used by heavier-than-air vehicles.

The range of the airship is greater if the altitude is low. Range in miles roughly follows a straight line function as shown below.

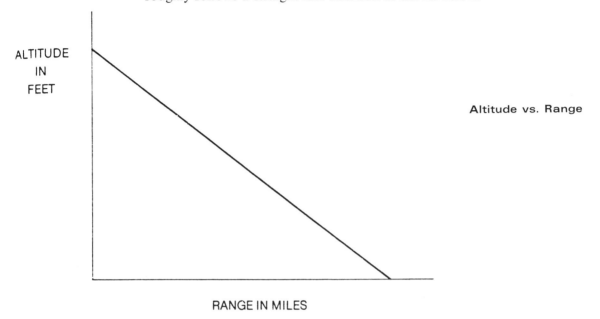

Altitude vs. Range

RANGE IN MILES

Endurance depends on the amount of fuel the airship can carry and its rate of consumption. However, the fuel consumption rate is related to the speed as shown below.

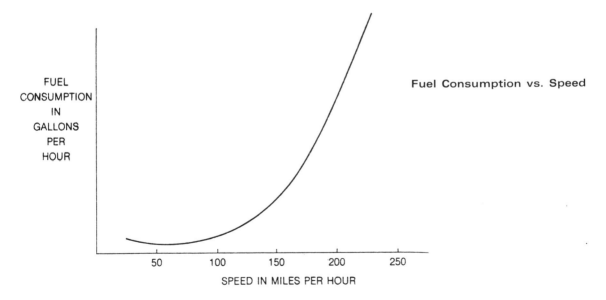

Fuel Consumption vs. Speed

SPEED IN MILES PER HOUR

From these studies, it's fairly simple to determine the most economical altitude and speed to operate the ship.

To be competitive in transporting cargo, the airship's cost per ton-mile must compare satisfactorily with trains and trucks or be below them; we already know that it is faster. Researchers at this point don't know exactly what the operational cost of the airship will be, due to variables which have not been determined since no large airship is operational. The chart below shows a general comparison of cost vs. speed.

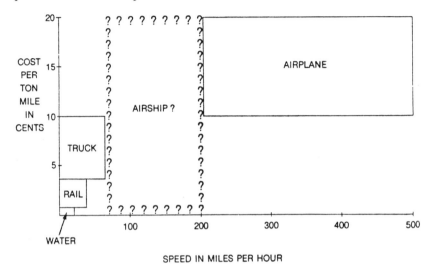

Cost vs. Speed

The basic unit of measurement in comparing various modes of transportation is cost per ton-mile. This is simply the cost of transporting one ton (0.9 tonne) in weight for a distance of one mile (1.6 kilometres). To arrive at this figure, the number of tons carried per year is compared with the total annual operating cost.

Speed plays a very important part in determining cost per ton-mile. The airplane travels from about 200 to over 500 miles (320 to over 800 kilometres) per hour and the cost per ton-mile is somewhere between 10 and 20 cents (6 and 12 pence). Truck, rail and water are less expensive but much slower. As you can see, there is a natural gap that the airship can fill. The design will determine its cost per ton-mile and what traffic it will capture.

Figuring on the basis of the same rate of utilization currently experienced by airline companies, the estimated cost per ton-mile looks very good to an investor. Airship enthusiasts within the aerospace industry expect the economical transportation of lightweight, large objects which take up too much room to be moved cheaply by airplane to provide a far better utilization rate for the airship, lowering costs even further. Another big estimate has to be made, though: the development cost and the cost per unit.

The development cost has to be considered because this eventually affects the cost per ton-mile. Normally, development cost of any new aircraft increases at a steady rate based on the size of the aircraft. For airships, gas capacity is used as the measurement of size.

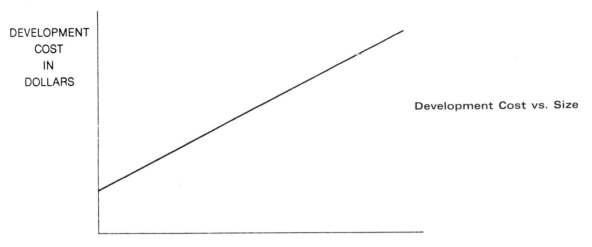

DEVELOPMENT COST IN DOLLARS

Development Cost vs. Size

GAS CAPACITY IN MILLION CUBIC FEET

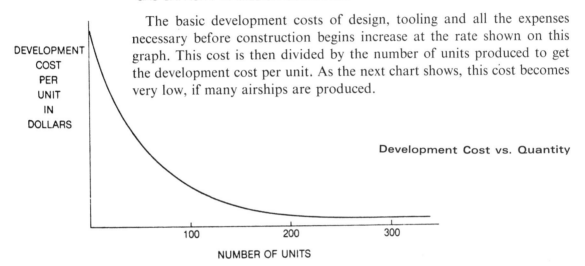

DEVELOPMENT COST PER UNIT IN DOLLARS

The basic development costs of design, tooling and all the expenses necessary before construction begins increase at the rate shown on this graph. This cost is then divided by the number of units produced to get the development cost per unit. As the next chart shows, this cost becomes very low, if many airships are produced.

Development Cost vs. Quantity

100   200   300

NUMBER OF UNITS

Production cost is another expense which a manufacturer must estimate. These costs are also similar to the experience of airplane manufacturers. The more units built, the cheaper production becomes (per unit) because of increased production efficiency.

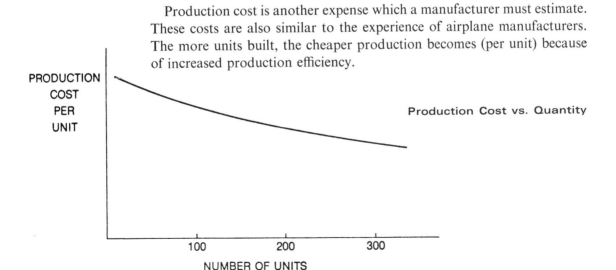

PRODUCTION COST PER UNIT

Production Cost vs. Quantity

100   200   300

NUMBER OF UNITS

Finally all of the discussed cost can be combined to estimate the overall cost of an airship.

Total Cost

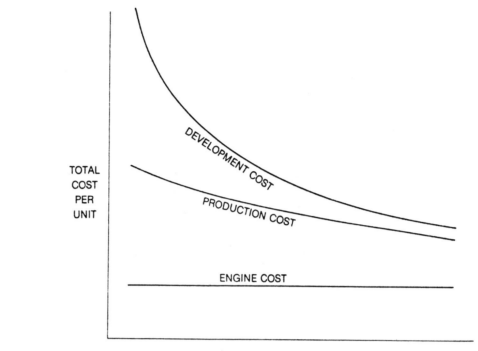

Recently, Morris B. Jobe, president of Goodyear Aerospace, stated "No single need provides the incentive for private development, but taken in total there is a national and worldwide need for economical, environmentally sound go-anywhere transportation that can be filled by airships." Judging from the best available sources, the airship can be designed to combine the many advantages of lighter-than-air flight in a vehicle which can compete economically with all of today's standard transportation systems.

IDEAS FOR THE FUTURE

The renewed interest in airships evident in the world today is no passing fad. The commercial and military potentials of the airship are tremendous. Technology, materials and know-how needed to provide airship solutions to the energy shortage, air and noise pollution, and the general dismal state of the transportation system exist today, but it will take a great deal of money to put all of the elements together into a working, practical airship transportation system. Many pioneering companies are currently at work to perfect airship technology with the very limited funds available to them. Some of the more promising designs, and a few that are actually being built, are presented in the following pages.

NON-RIGID DESIGNS AND CONCEPTS

WDL

Westdeutsche Luftwerbung (WDL) of West Germany is currently engaged in a developmental program aimed at the construction of a standard production model non-rigid airship designed to handle a payload of 33

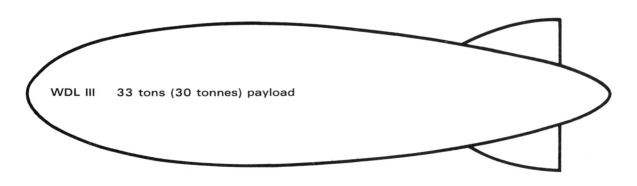

WDL III   33 tons (30 tonnes) payload

STANDARD AIRSHIP
Volume: 2,240,000 cubic feet (64,000 cubic metres)
Length: 400 feet (120 metres)
Gross Weight: 46,000 pounds (21,000 kilograms)
Power Units: 2, each 700 horsepower
Payload: 66,000 pounds (30,000 kilograms)
Maximum Speed: 87 miles (140 kilometres) per hour
Range: 5,300 miles (8,600 kilometres) or more

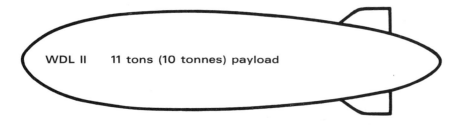

WDL II   11 tons (10 tonnes) payload

DEVELOPMENTAL MODEL II
Volume: 700,000 cubic feet (20,000 cubic metres)
Length: 265 feet (80 metres)
Gross Weight: 46,000 pounds (21,000 kilograms)
Power Units: 2, each 400 horsepower
Payload: 22,000 pounds (10,000 kilograms)
Maximum Speed: 87 miles (140 kilometres) per hour
Range: 1,500 miles (2,400 kilometres)

WDL I   3,300 lbs.
(1,500 kg.) payload

DEVELOPMENTAL MODEL I
Volume: 210,000 cubic feet (6,000 cubic metres)
Length: 200 feet (60 metres)
Gross Weight: 13,850 pounds (6,300 kilograms)
Payload: 3,300 pounds (1,500 kilograms)
Maximum Speed: 60 miles (100 kilometres) per hour
Range: 4,000 miles (1,800 kilometres)

tons (30 tonnes). Their work has not been limited to design drawings, though. They have already built three non-rigids in their WDL I series, two of which have been sold to Japanese companies. The helium-filled WDL I is similar in many respects to the familiar Goodyear blimp, including the use of thousands of electric light bulbs to convey advertising messages at night.

The WDL I is approximately 200 feet (60 metres) long and has a volume of over 200,000 cubic feet (6,000 cubic metres). The ship is propelled by two 180-horsepower engines drawing their fuel from storage tanks located within the envelope to maximize available space in the gondola. The first flight of WDL I occurred in 1972 in an airship named *The Flying Musketeer,* which is still flying today under a different name, *Wicküler*.

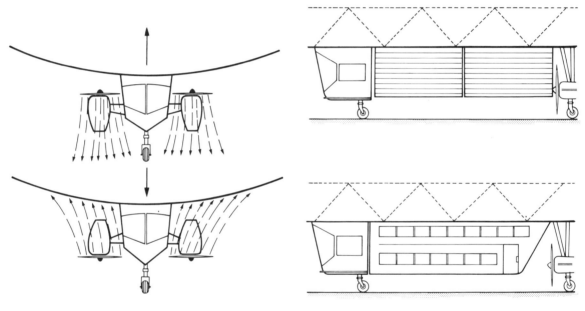

WDL is working on an innovative engine suspension to provide additional vertical control.

The development of a standardized interchangeable gondola system will allow increased speed of handling for cargo and passengers.

The next developmental craft, WDL II, is currently being designed. It will incorporate several innovative procedures. The gondola is being designed to permit use and transport of the standard-sized containers employed for international freight traffic. The easy interchange of cargo containers and passenger gondolas will make the airship more economical by cutting the time needed to load and unload freight, and allow the same airship to switch quickly from passenger to cargo hauling operations.

Another innovation is the development of an engine suspension system which will enable the power units to be rotated 360 degrees, providing additional lifting power when called for.

The gondola framework of WDL I (left) and the completed gondola construction (right).

Aerospace Developments

Aerospace Developments, the same company involved in designing a natural gas tanker airship for Shell International, is designing a range of non-rigid airships. An order has been received from Venezuela for a prototype with a volume of about 170,000 cubic feet (4,800 cubic metres) capable of carrying 10 people. The airship, which will be used for passenger transport and for advertising, is now in the design stage. If successful, it is expected that a further order for production airships will be placed. It has been suggested that this could be for over 20 ships.

The HASPA vehicle will provide an airborne platform at 70,000 feet (21,000 metres) over a fixed station for up to 30 days.

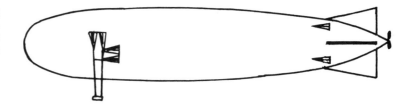

HASPA

The Martin-Marietta Corporation, in association with Sheldahl, Inc., is building an unmanned non-rigid to operate at 70,000 feet (21,000 metres) for over-the-horizon surveillance. The project is known as HASPA (High Altitude Superpressure Powered Aerostat). The design stresses high operational altitude and low flight speed, with the propulsion unit located at the stern.

Police Blimp

In 1974, Goodyear Aerospace Corporation conducted a six-month study for the city of Tempe, Arizona, evaluating the feasibility of employing two-man blimps as silent crime fighters. The study concluded that non-rigids somewhat smaller than the Goodyear blimp could be built for as little as $520,000 each to serve as aerial platforms for police surveillance and crime control. The blimps, which could fly as low as 500 feet (150 metres) off the ground, would require a one-man ground crew, and the operating costs would compare favorably with the operating costs for police helicopters. The blimp would cruise at approximately 40 miles (64 kilometres) per hour, carrying a pilot and an observer, binoculars, cameras, spotlights, radios, loudspeakers, sirens, guns and ammunition.

The streets of Bell Gardens, California, will reportedly be patrolled in the future by small manned airships about one third the size of the present Goodyear blimps. The Chief of Police feels that the airship can do many more things than the helicopters now being used. The patrols will lead to monetary savings also, since the airship is expected to cost $10 an hour to operate, against $130 an hour for helicopters.

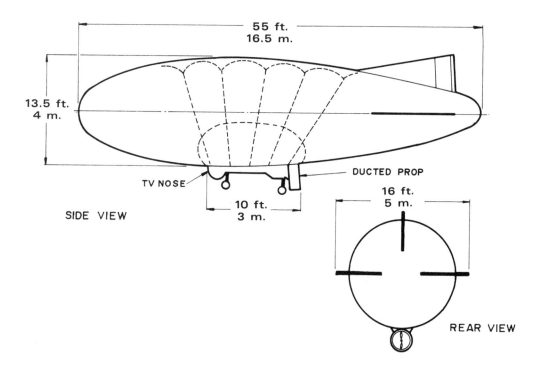

55 ft.
16.5 m.

13.5 ft.
4 m.

TV NOSE

DUCTED PROP

10 ft.
3 m.

SIDE VIEW

16 ft.
5 m.

REAR VIEW

Remotely Piloted Mini-Blimps

Developmental Sciences Inc. in California has flown a prototype of a small surveillance blimp which employs the type of radio control gear now used in model airplanes to provide remote control. The company has presented its plan to law enforcement officials as a means for surveying traffic problems and environmental disturbances, and patrolling large areas with minimal manpower. Each RPMB can carry a small television camera and transmitter which links it with a central control, and the flight func-

The prototype RPMB has been flown for demonstration to law enforcement officials.

A typical car for the RPMB includes a lightweight propulsion unit and compact television camera.

tions are simple enough so that one man can keep several blimps flying simultaneously.

Figures prepared by Developmental Sciences indicate that, though the initial price of each blimp would be approximately the same as a helicopter, operating costs would be substantially lower due to lower maintenance and personnel costs. The craft is a splendid example of adapting current technology to meet rising needs. The television equipment and the lightweight materials for construction all exist today in other fields, and the propulsion system is spun off from the motorcycle and snowmobile industries. A number of government and private organizations, including the Coast Guard, the Environmental Protection Agency, the Federal Highway Administration and many city, state, and county officials have expressed interest in the RPMB, and the manufacturer expects full-scale development and demonstration to commence early in 1977.

Dynastat

This Goodyear proposal has a shape somewhat similar to the familiar blimp, but flatter and wider. This shape gives it the winglike characteristics of the deltoid class, with improved manoeuvring and load-carrying capabilities. The helium-filled craft would be either non-rigid or semi-rigid and capable of VTOL.

This Cameron D-96 hot-air airship was delivered to a customer in Louisville, Kentucky in February, 1976.

HOT-AIR AIRSHIPS

Cameron Balloons

The first lifting gas employed in balloons was simply hot air, and today this plentiful supply of lifting power is being tapped by two companies, Cameron Balloons and Raven Industries, both actively engaged in the manufacture of hot-air airships.

Cameron Balloons Ltd., located in Bristol, England, flew the world's first hot-air airship on January 7, 1973. The 100-foot- (30.5-metre-) long craft carries two men in a lightweight gondola which also houses the propane-powered Volkswagen engine and twin burner unit for inflating the envelope with hot air. Even the fins are air-inflated, and the whole envelope packs neatly into a large balloon bag when deflated.

Cameron's award-winning design has now entered production, and is available in England and the United States. While primarily designed for advertising and publicity uses, this ship has low vibration flight characteristics that might provide a better platform for surveying and photography than a helicopter, the manufacturer suggests.

The Raven STAR ship in a tethered buoyancy test.

Raven Industries

Raven Industries in South Dakota has built a manned thermal airship with a useful lift of 500 pounds (225 kilograms) and a three-hour duration in the air. Its first flight was in January, 1975, powered by a single 75-horsepower Volkswagen engine. The aluminum frame of the gondola is covered with fabric, and is large enough to contain pilot and co-pilot, both propane for the burners and aviation fuel for the motors, and a full complement of aviation instruments and radio equipment. In addition to use as a flying advertising billboard, the vehicle is expected to be useful as an observation platform for environmental monitoring, traffic control and search and rescue operations.

The Raven prototype airship is now in regular commercial operation, serving as an advertising billboard for a Minnesota bank, and has flown

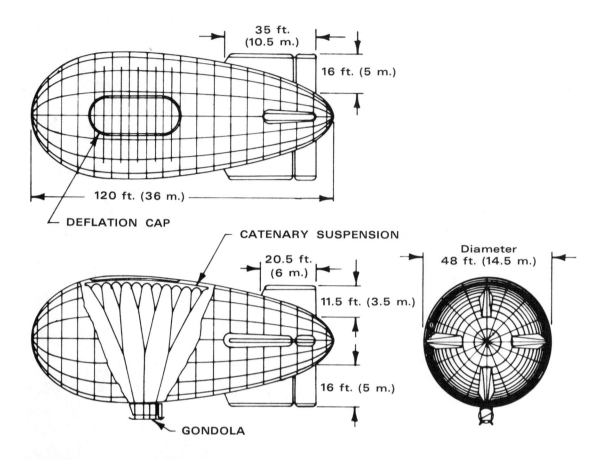

35 ft.
(10.5 m.)

16 ft. (5 m.)

120 ft. (36 m.)

DEFLATION CAP

CATENARY SUSPENSION

20.5 ft.
(6 m.)

11.5 ft. (3.5 m.)

16 ft. (5 m.)

Diameter
48 ft. (14.5 m.)

GONDOLA

Left, the Revmaster VW engine and Maloof metal propeller installed in the rear of the gondola. Above, a front view of the gondola.

The Raven prototype flying over Minneapolis. Note that even the rudder and elevator at the rear of the airship are inflatable.

in the Minneapolis-St. Paul area an average of more than once a week during the last half of 1977.

The most important design change being planned is a model with a 20 per cent larger envelope.

The instrument panel includes the main engine instruments in the left panel, rate of rise, temperature control, autopilot, altimeter and envelope pressure gauge in the middle panel and fuel and airspeed indicators in the right panel.

Aerosport

Aerosport, a Buenos Aires firm, has been authorized by the Argentine Air Force to design and construct a hot-air airship. This will be the first of its type in Latin America. It is based on an original design by Gilberto Julian Riega. Construction was underway at the time of writing, and completion was expected in "early 1978."

The ship will be 144.3 feet (44 metres) long and have a capacity of 209,415 cubic feet (5,926 cubic metres). The maximum lift has been calculated at over 4,200 pounds (1,900 kilograms), and a crew of four is planned.

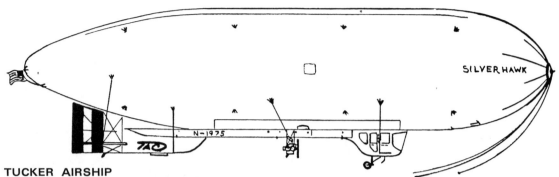

TUCKER AIRSHIP

Length:	91 feet (27 metres)
Total Height:	26 feet (8 metres)
Volume:	20,500 cubic feet (615 cubic metres)
Maximum Lift, Sea Level:	1,400 pounds (630 kilograms)
Payload and Disposable Weights:	750 pounds (338 kilograms)
Fuel Consumption:	5 gallons (19 litres) per hour
Top Air Speed:	55 miles (88 kilometres) per hour
Cruising Speed:	0—45 miles (72 kilometres) per hour
Fuel Tanks/Range:	Maximum 60 gallons (228 litres)/500 miles (800 kilometres)

SEMI-RIGID CONSTRUCTION

Tucker Airship

Currently under construction in Los Angeles, California, the TX-1 is a semi-rigid design. The design of the ship is extremely simple in order to fulfill its rôle as a laboratory to flight test new design, material and ground-handling concepts. The TX-1 would also make a suitable trainer vehicle for LTA pilots, and will be made available to scientific, military and industrial organizations upon request.

The ship will be 91 feet (27 metres) long and have a range of 500 miles (800 kilometres) with a pilot and a passenger. The entire structure can be separated into 12 units and carried by a single trailer, adding to the portability and low storage costs of the vehicle. The TX-1 was designed to operate safely for short test periods with inexpensive hydrogen as a lifting gas, but for periods exceeding five days the envelope will be filled with helium.

A test mating of the envelope with the lower framework.

Construction of TX-1 is well advanced, and the builders hope to be airborne shortly.

Outside funding for the TX-1 has ceased, but the project is still alive thanks to the determination of the company president. A new larger 120 hp engine is being tested, and a design has been completed for a double-wall, air-inflated hangar, measuring 110 x 40 x 35 feet (33.5 x 12.2 x 10.7 metres). The hangar will feature an air-operated clamshell door which will swing upwards, and will be portable for TX-1 field maintenance.

The gondola and rigid keel structure.

Plans for a natural gas tanker airship call for a stainless steel sandwich with a Kevlar core for the hull material.

RIGID DESIGNS AND CONCEPTS

Natural Gas Tanker

Aerospace Developments Ltd. of London has spent over a million dollars investigating for the Shell Oil Company the possible development of a tanker version of a giant airship to be used to transport natural gas. The 1,800-foot- (550-metre-) long airship will have a capacity of 100,000,000 cubic feet (2,830,000 cubic metres). The overall shape is fairly conventional, but new materials and structural techniques will be employed. A flexible membrane will separate air and gas within the hull.

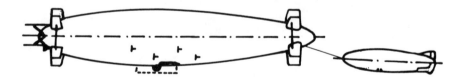

Proposed heavy-lift airship with "fuel-blimp."

Airfloat Transport

Airfloat Transport Ltd. has been studying a novel rigid airship configuration since 1970. The company proposes to mount propulsion and steering units both forward and aft to provide improved control in the air. A separate "fuel-blimp" will carry gaseous fuel for the 10 turboprop engines. Airfloat Transport is studying many innovative possibilities, including the use of heated helium at take-off, which is permitted to cool as fuel is consumed. One of their most exciting proposals is the possibility of loading and unloading cargo while the airship is hovering. This would be a tremendous breakthrough since this would give airships the ability to deliver cargo exactly where it is needed to a much greater degree than is possible with airplanes.

Cargo Airships

Cargo Airship Ltd. has proposed use of large rigid airships in a freight transport rôle. Their airship would be built along conventional rigid airship lines with a capacity of 40,000,000 cubic feet (1,100,000 cubic metres). They are particularly interested in the airship's suitability for carrying vast amounts of refrigerated cargo.

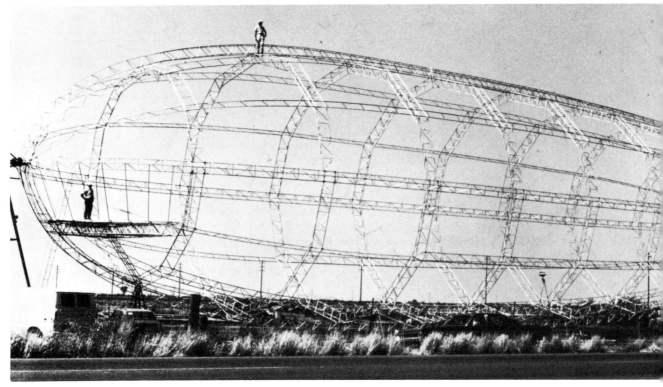

Mr. C. W. Conrad atop the framework for **CA 220** in the Arizona desert.

Conrad Airships

One of the most interesting companies on the LTA scene is Conrad Airship Corporation of Mesa, Arizona. The company was founded by C. W. Conrad, a pilot of heavier-than-air craft for 30 years, who believes that the time has come to begin actual construction of an airship using modern materials and techniques. With the help of his son, Darwin, he began construction of the huge rigid framework for the CA 220, a 225-foot- (67.5-metre-) long craft designed to receive lift from 10 helium-filled gas cells and propulsion from three internally-mounted engines for a speed of 80 miles (125 kilometres) per hour.

The framework was virtually completed and the Conrads and crew were preparing to begin attaching a mylar covering when, on July 16, 1975, a wind of tornado force roared out of the Arizona desert. The framework was severely damaged at its outdoor construction site. The dejected builders were pleasantly surprised, though, when the resulting publicity brought cash contributions and offers of volunteer labor from local sources.

The Conrads are building again, hoping to attract enough contributions to complete their 30-passenger dirigible. This overriding project has not consumed all of Mr. Conrad's seemingly boundless energy, though. He has built several prototype models, including a fully buoyant hydrogen-filled airship 24 feet (7.3 metres) long. A more current project is a flying-saucer-shaped LTA vehicle 80 feet (24 metres) in diameter and approximately 26 feet (8 metres) high. The framework has been completed, the covering is on order and is now being laminated. The engines are ready now, and the gas cells are on order. A firm target date for completion has not been set, although Mr. Conrad has stated that early 1978 is a possibility. He feels the saucer will "cause a considerable stir when it is flying."

The finished framework for the flying-saucer airship will have 48 arching frames. Propulsion units will be mounted front and back for greater manoeuvrability.

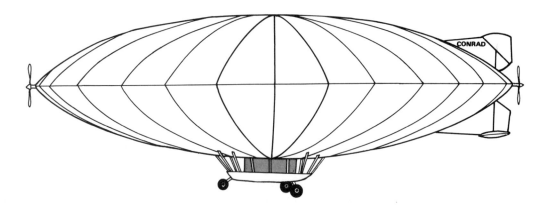

One proposed use of the Airship Advertising craft is high altitude surveying of the earth's surface. The company now expects to go into production in 1977.

Airship Advertising

Airship Advertising Inc. of Cape May, New Jersey has an application on file with the Federal Aviation Administration to obtain a flight certificate for a giant rigid airship. The company planned to build a rigid along conventional lines to be used for massive advertising and for geophysical survey work. Construction began on the 248-foot (75-metre) standard design, but at this time work has been interrupted due to a shortage of money. However, the initial work has not been destroyed, and construction is expected to continue.

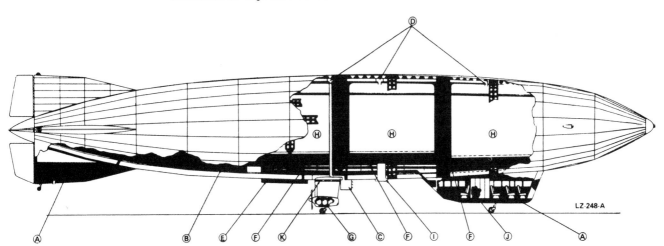

A. Water Ballast
B. Water Ballast Transfer System
C. Air Conditioning Unit
D. Air Conditioning Transfer Units
E. Heating Unit
F. Heating Transfer Units

G. 6-cylinder, 300-horsepower Engines
H. Gas Container
I. Helium Pressure Release Valve
J. 100 Amp. Generator System
K. Wing Assembly Dampening Unit

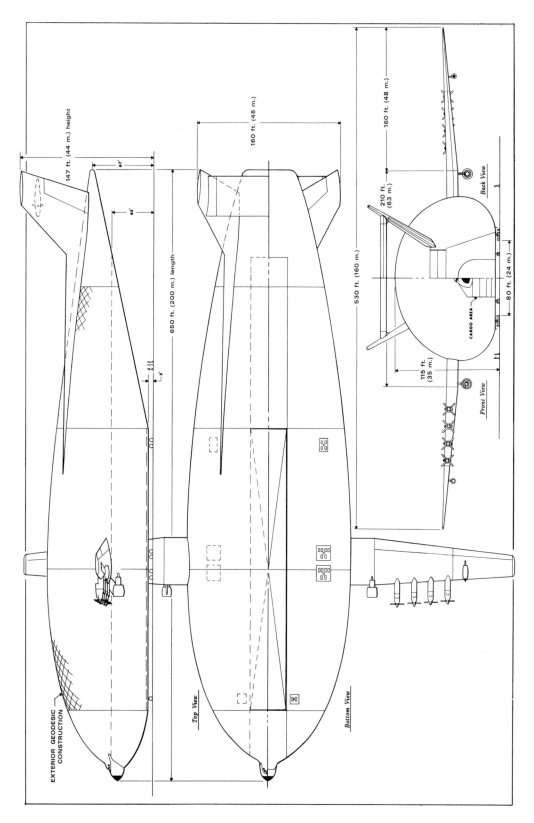

EXTERIOR GEODESIC
CONSTRUCTION

147 ft. (44 m.) height

67°

43°

6'

5'

650 ft. (200 m.) length

Top View

160 ft. (48 m.)

Bottom View

530 ft. (160 m.)

160 ft. (48 m.)

Back View

210 ft.
(63 m.)

80 ft. (24 m.)

CARGO AREA

Front View

115 ft.
(35 m.)

132

A mock-up of the Megalifter compared in size with the cargo aircraft C-5A.

Megalifter

The Megalifter concept is a true hybrid of airship and airplane technologies. The Megalifter Company proposes the incorporation of a helium-filled envelope with a conventional lifting wing. The lifting gas would cancel out a major portion of the initial airframe dead weight,

The shaded portion of this diagram indicates the space for helium compartments in the Megalifter design.

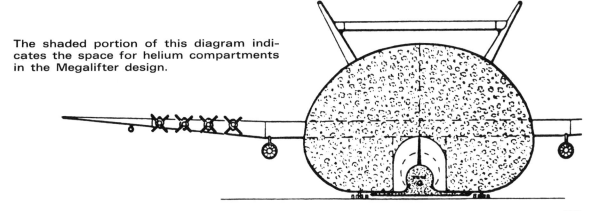

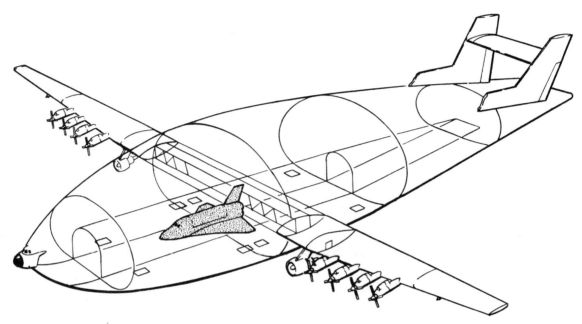

The cargo compartment could be adapted for launching of small aircraft over selected targets.

allowing short take-off and landing capability and substantial fuel savings while cruising.

The proposed ship would be built from components of existing U.S. Air Force aircraft, cutting to a minimum the time and expense required for building the vehicle. It would contain nine helium cells to provide the buoyancy needed to carry a payload of 400,000 pounds (180,000 kilograms). The estimated cruising speed is 205 miles (330 kilometres) per hour at an altitude of 18,000 feet (5,400 metres). One of the more interesting proposed applications of the Megalifter, in addition to cargo transport, is the possibility of employing the vehicle as a mobile missile launch station. The cargo compartment could be adapted for vertical storage of ICBM missile hardware for drop/launch from the air. It has been calculated that a Megalifter could remain aloft without refueling for 62 hours with four Minuteman missiles as cargo while flying at airspeeds as low as 75 miles (120 kilometres) per hour for a distance of over 7,800 miles (12,500 kilometres).

Nuclear-Powered Airships

The possibility of maintaining a constant weight during an airship flight by replacing conventional fuel sources with a nuclear powerplant holds great promise for the airships of the future. Professor Francis Morse of Boston University has proposed a nuclear-powered conventional rigid. A propeller mounted at the tail end of the ship would provide propulsion.

134

This artist's conception of a passenger-carrying nuclear-powered airship, reflecting a rigid airship design proposed by Professor Morse, shows the propulsion details enlarged for clarity.

There are reports that the Soviet Union is developing a nuclear-powered airship capable of carrying a payload of 180 tons (162 tonnes) or 1,800 passengers at a speed of 190 miles (300 kilometres) per hour.

The U.S. Navy's metalclad ZMC-2.

Metalclad Concepts

The Southern California Aviation Council has plans to build a modernized version of the ZMC-2, a metalclad airship which operated successfully for 11 years as a U.S. Navy craft. The new ship will feature an Alclad covering with light framing to protect the structure when depressurized between flights.

The Slate SMD-100 is another proposed metalclad vehicle. This ship will carry a 25-man crew and immense loads slung close up to the underside of the envelope at speeds up to 100 miles (160 kilometres) per hour. It could be either jet- or nuclear-powered, with the control room and passenger accommodations located in the lower tail fin.

The successful flight test of Aereon 26 at N.A.F.E.C., Atlantic City, New Jersey on March 6, 1971. (Copyright © 1975, Aereon Corporation)

HYBRID DESIGNS AND CONCEPTS

Aereon

One of the earliest and most avid proponents of modern airship design is the Aereon Corporation of Princeton, New Jersey. Founded in 1959, Aereon has invested well over a million dollars of private funds over the years to advance the art of aeronautical technology. The first major Aereon construction was the experimental airship Aereon III, a triple-hulled vehicle built in 1963. At that time it was the only rigid airship built and tested in the United States since the 1930's.

The triple-hulled Aereon III did not survive ground testing.

Aereon III resembled a large elongated flying wing. It was 86 feet (26 metres) long, 18 feet (5.5 metres) high and 53 feet (16 metres) wide, with an uninflated weight of 2,700 pounds (1,226 kilograms). The three elongated hulls each contained six helium-filled cells for a total of 40,000 cubic feet (1,132 cubic metres) of lifting gas. The design called for a stern propulsion unit, but the vehicle was never flight tested. Propulsion was provided by a two-bladed helicopter for ground testing.

The stern propeller (left) and control cabin (right) of Aereon III.

The triple-hull design of Aereon III proved unsound, the result of inadequate engineering and construction experience. The craft suffered an accident during ground testing and was finally dismantled completely in 1967. The Aereon company continued research and development with a new concept, a delta-shaped aerobody. The designers employed a computer optimization study using facilities of the G.E. Space Center at Valley Forge, Pennsylvania, to arrive at an aerodynamically sound configuration. The resulting craft, Aereon 26, has been described as a "deltoid pumpkin seed," a bright orange triangular ship which combines the lift

The flight tests of Aereon 26 proved the lifting capability of the deltoid shape without helium. (Copyright © 1973, Aereon Corporation)

of the wing shape with the capacity for additional lift from helium cells in the hull. Aereon 26 is an experimental craft which proved the feasibility of the basic shape and design through a series of successful manned flights without helium in 1971.

A perfect landing at N.A.F.E.C. during 1971 flight testing. (Copyright © 1975, Aereon Corporation)

The full-size deltoid airship would carry large cargos economically.

Aereon 26 is 27 feet (8 metres) long with a gross weight of 1,200 pounds (545 kilograms). It has accumulated about four hours of air-time and many hours of runway and ground testing, proving itself stable and controllable within acceptable margins. The craft is currently hangared in New Jersey on standby status.

Several versions of the Aereon delta-wing concept have been proposed since 1967. The Aereon 340 resembles a large fat flying triangle, 340 feet (100 metres) long with a wing span of 256 feet (77 metres). It was conceived as a vehicle for commercial freight transport, capable of handling standard size inter-modal containers. Propulsion would be achieved with four 5,500-horsepower Rolls Royce Tyne Turbo-Prop engines mounted in the rear. The helium gas would be carried internally in large individual envelopes which would make the Aereon 340 nearly as light as air. The cargo area would have built-in cargo-handling equipment and would accommodate six fully loaded trailers or trailer size containers. Aereon projected a five-man crew to operate the big carrier.

Studies have been done under contract for the U.S. Navy to develop the Dynairship for oceanic surveillance. This craft would be 600 feet (180 metres) long, with the ability to remain airborne for several days at a time, flying slowly near the ocean surface, but capable of a speed of 230 miles (370 kilometres) per hour if required. It would be nearly buoyant, but could carry heavy loads due to its lifting-hull shape.

The Aer/lighter is a concept designed for a variety of missions which require capabilities similar to a helicopter but offering greater range, more

The Aer/lighter vehicle would be capable of V/STOL operation with heavy loads. (Copyright © 1975, Aereon Corporation)

cargo space and lower energy consumption. It is expected to be about 260 feet (78 metres) long and combine VTOL (vertical take-off and landing) and STOL (short take-off and landing) capabilities. Aereon is currently considering applications in remote area logistics, long endurance surveillance and passenger flights.

The design team is currently engaged in reevaluating this configuration.

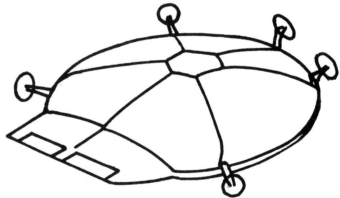

Skyship

The design of the Skyship project currently being studied by Skyship Transport Ltd. in England looks distinctly like the elusive UFO or flying saucer. It is a lens-shaped rigid structure with 19 helium compartments to provide buoyancy. The proposed vehicle would be able to carry a massive payload in the central core, a layout considered to be more efficient structurally and aerodynamically than the familiar sausage-shaped airship by the designers. Imperial College (London) and British Hovercraft

Corporation are co-operating with Skyship Ltd. on the project. A prototype 30 feet (13.6 metres) in diameter was recently flown in Cardington, England.

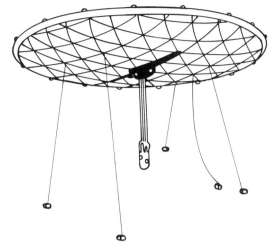

The C.N.R.S. lens-shaped airship.

Atlas

The Atlas project is the latest stage in a continuing investigation by a group of French manufacturers led by the Centre National de la Recherche Scientifique (C.N.R.S.) into the characteristics of lens-shaped airships. The original developmental stage was the Pegase platform designed to serve as a high-altitude telecommunications relay system. Further studies grew out of this, including the Titan crane concept designed for short- and medium-distance flights with heavy indivisible payloads. The current Atlas program has two primary goals: a progressive increase in volume and the development of a number of uses for the same basic airship.

The Obelix concept merges helicopter and balloon technologies for a heavy-lift vehicle.

Obelix

The Obelix Flying Crane is a French concept which uses four balloons, each with a capacity of nearly 8,000,000 cubic feet (743,000 cubic metres) to which six or eight helicopter rotors are attached using an open frame support structure. It is designed to carry loads of 500 tons (450 tonnes) over relatively short distances. The design team believes that the vehicle could be flying within five years if concentrated research and development activities began immediately.

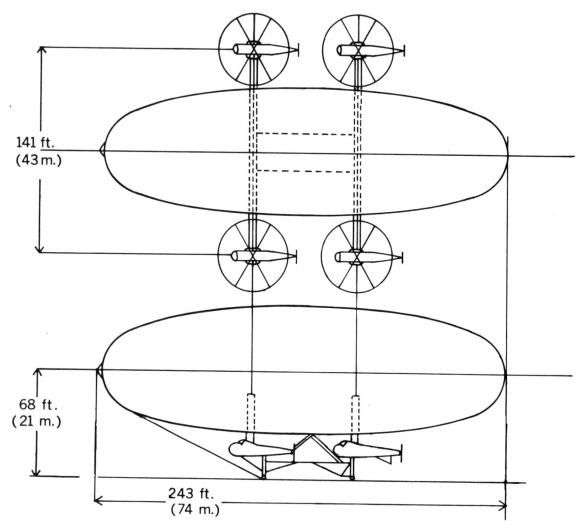

141 ft.
(43 m.)

68 ft.
(21 m.)

243 ft.
(74 m.)

Heli-Stat prototype configuration with four CH-34 helicopters attached.

Heli-Stat

Piasecki Aircraft Corporation of Philadelphia is performing a design analysis of a new hybrid airship called the Heli-Stat under U.S. Navy contract. This system employs existing technology to produce an efficient system for ultra-heavy lift by attaching four large helicopters to a structural frame which forms the base of a tremendous helium-filled rigid structure similar to the hull of earlier rigid airships.

The project is now beyond the investigation stage, reports company president Frank Piasecki, who is preparing to build a 243-foot (73-metre) prototype. Cargo space will be provided in the central keel with a projected volume of 6,700 cubic feet (200 cubic metres). The envelope of

Heli-Stat mock-up

the prototype will have a capacity of 1,000,000 cubic feet (30,000 cubic metres), making the entire vehicle buoyant when not loaded. The aerostat will provide lift to support the weight of the entire assembly, including the helicopters. The helicopters then will supply the lift to support the payload, as well as provide propulsion and control to enable the Heli-Stat to hover with precision, an impossibility with conventional airships.

The power plant will consist of four Sikorsky CH-34 helicopters, each powered by a Wright piston engine rated at 1,525 bhp. The rigid structure supporting the envelope and connecting with the helicopters and landing gear will all be made of light alloy, to keep weight down for economical operation.

One of the four helicopters, of the type in use today, will serve as the master control station, with pilots ready in the other three in case of emergency. A recent computer study of a Heli-Stat vehicle consisting of four Sikorsky CH-53D helicopters and an aerostat of 3,600,000 cubic feet (100,000 cubic metres) showed the control power capable of holding a hovering position within 6 inches (15 centimetres) in gusts up to 50 feet (15 metres) per second. This degree of accuracy would bring new economy to massive construction projects. Time for overland transportation of oversize structures and equipment could be drastically reduced. Oil drill rigs, powerplants, boilers, chemical process vessels and sections of bridges could be preassembled by the manufacturer and sent directly from the factory to be placed on foundations and attachment points. The same vehicle would be suitable for cargo transportation to undeveloped ports as well as for military logistical missions.

Among the varied applications of an Aerocrane vehicle would be fighting fires in high-rise buildings or forests, and delivery of heavy equipment.

Aerocrane

The U.S. Navy has awarded a contract of $85,000 to the All American Engineering Company of Wilmington, Delaware, to study a vehicle known as the Aerocrane. The Aerocrane is a hybrid model which basically consists of a large spherical balloon with four rotors attached to it at 90-degree intervals. The entire structure rotates at approximately 10 revolutions per minute, combining the lift provided by the four wings with the lift of the helium gas in the sphere. The control cab or gondola is located directly below the vertical centerline of the sphere. The pilot will have at this station all necessary engine and flight controls, navigation equipment, radio equipment and all life-support systems. The proposed vehicle would be capable of lifting 70 tons (63 tonnes) and transporting this load at a speed of 42 miles (68 kilometres) per hour. The cost of moving cargo at payload capacity has been calculated as one fourth that for a comparable helicopter or a Boeing 747 jumbo jet. The company has built a small model of the Aerocrane which, while heavier-than-air, illustrates the fundamental principles involved in the concept.

Tests conducted at Princeton University continue to add support to the Aerocrane concept. Free-flight tests have been conducted with the 16-foot- (5-metre-) diameter balloon with a 40-foot (12-metre) wingspan shown on page 145. Forward flight tests have also been conducted. The test data from this program, along with the earlier hover flight test data,

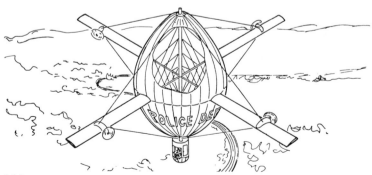

An Aerocrane surveillance vehicle would be capable of extended stationary hovering.

Prototype Aerocrane vehicle.

matched the theoretical expectations very closely. As a result, All American now states that they understand quite well the aeronautical and flight technologies of a winglet, spherical Aerocrane, and have the basic flight dynamics well in hand.

The areas of flight control, propulsion, structural design, construction and ground handling are all at a point where no major problems are foreseen. Testing is still underway to evaluate the Aerocrane's performance in wind and at high tilt angles, to establish extreme manoeuvre boundaries and to achieve optimum winglet performance.

Comprehensive economic studies of short haul heavy-lift markets are also being conducted, principally in the U.S. and Canada. If this testing indicates potential economic success, All American will proceed with the manufacture and deployment of a fleet of Aerocranes.

At present, the timetable calls for completion of a prototype 12 to 16 ton (11 to 14.5 tonne) slingload vehicle by mid-1980, with construction beginning sometime in 1979. The actual construction will be done by a major aerospace contractor. Flight tests would then be completed by early 1981, and a commercially exploitable 16 to 20 ton (14.5 to 18 tonne) slingload Aerocrane could be introduced in mid or late 1982.

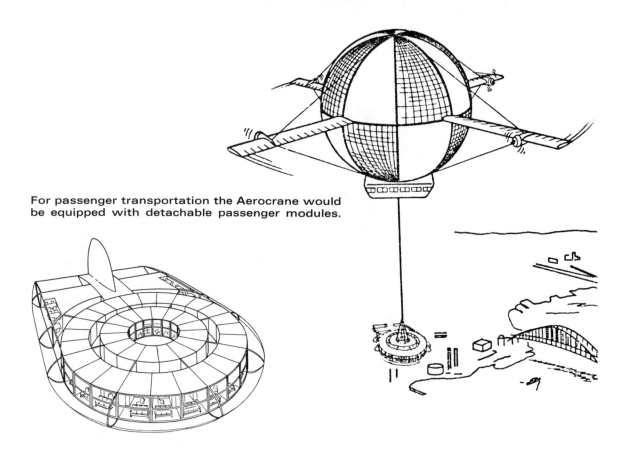

For passenger transportation the Aerocrane would be equipped with detachable passenger modules.

Of course, if Canada, England or Russia, all of whom are known to be developing heavy-lift vehicles, complete their own testing successfully, All American's schedule would probably be moved up dramatically.

Helipsoid

The Helipsoid concept was chosen by Boeing Vertol Company as the best compromise shape for a moderately high speed airship considering optimum structural, aerodynamic and control requirements along with a compact lifting body. It would be most likely suited to a rigid structure with a multicell arrangement. The design endeavors to reduce length and height to facilitate manufacture and hangaring as well as better matching the typical helicopter landing pad. This is a partially buoyant VTOL concept.

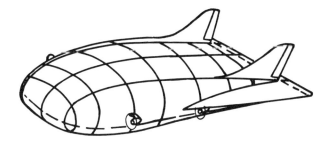

Deltoid

The Boeing Deltoid concept is a hybrid. The body structure would be a rigid-type construction with a multicell lifting gas arrangement. The inboard engines would drive prop-rotors which could be directed for angle of thrust. This design could be either VTOL or STOL. It would have lowest operating cost and greatest cargo-carrying capacity at low altitudes cruising at a speed of 95 to 120 miles (150 to 200 kilometres) per hour.

Other International Activity

Continuing efforts by governmental agencies to draft guidelines for evaluating airship flight safety reflect official recognition of the growing airship movement. The Civil Aviation Authority, the British equivalent of the U.S. Federal Aviation Administration, has issued Paper No. 708, a working draft of "British Civil Airworthiness Requirements for Non-Rigid Airships." The Canadian Ministry of Transport and Civil Aeronautics had earlier released their provisional "Requirements for Airships."

The British proposals are applicable to non-rigid, multi-piston-engined airships, inflated with a nonflammable gas, with a maximum inflated envelope volume not greater than 1,500,000 cubic feet (45,000 cubic metres).

Unlike the British regulations specifically for smaller non-rigid airships, the Canadian regulations cover non-rigid, semi-rigid and rigid airships, and place no limit on the envelope volume. They do, however, require that the lifting gas be nonflammable.

In April 1978, the U.S. Federal Aviation Administration finally acknowledged the actual and potential activity in the airship field. In their order "Airworthiness Certification of Aircraft and Related Approvals," airships will be added to the paragraph dealing with assigned areas for flight testing. This is a first step to eventual F.A.A. regulations covering airships.

"Jane's Freight Containers" indicates that the Soviet Union, East and West Germany, the Netherlands and France have plans on the drawing board for new airship projects.

Defense sources in England report that the Royal Navy hopes to use miniblimps to patrol Britain's expanded fishing waters and its 985-billion-dollar North Sea oil assets. Builders claim that a fleet of six such dirigibles could provide the necessary surveillance at a fraction of the cost of the ships and planes now being used. Aerospace Development has called the new blimp the AD-500. The proposed airship would be 164 feet (50 metres) long, use 180,000 cubic feet (5,400 cubic metres) of helium, travel at 70 miles (110 kilometres) per hour and have a range of 1,500 miles (2,400 kilometres).

The cost is estimated at $600,000 each and it will cost about $45 an hour to operate each blimp, compared with the $1200 per hour it costs to operate the Nimrod anti-submarine aircraft currently being used.

The U.S. Naval Air Development Center awarded a $60,000 contract to Goodyear Aerospace to study a modernized version of the ZPG-3W non-rigid airship.

Flugschiffbau Hamburg and Unimar of West Germany are proposing short and medium range rigid airships for passengers and freight operations. These ships would have a volume in the 7,000,000 cubic foot (200,000 cubic metre) range.

Soviet News Agency Tass reported that plans have been approved for construction of a mile-long balloon "Sky-Train" to carry petroleum products. This proposal is similar to an early idea advanced by Airship Advertising.

Reliable sources have reported that the Soviets are testing a balloon-like crane vehicle for heavy-lift operations.

Lightspeed Collective, a European group, is promoting a new variation of the dirigible in the United States.

Unimar Seatransport of Hamburg, West Germany, is studying the airship's application for long-haul cargo transport.

Schlichting Shipbuilding Company of Lubeck-Travemuende, West Germany, is doing a feasibility study of a plastic-skin helium-filled rigid airship using nuclear propulsion.

The Canadian Airship Development Corporation in Ontario has built a small non-rigid prototype ship 120 feet (36 metres) long to gain training and operational experience before embarking on development of large commercial airships.

Combustion Engineering of Hartford, Connecticut, has entered an agreement with a large aerospace company to study jointly the airship as a method for moving large nuclear powerplant components.

conclusion

At present, as in former times, scientific knowledge is at the mercy of balloons—globes lighter than air and therefore the sport and the prey of tempests and currents.

          – Ascents,1870

Since an airship is essentially a balloon which has been outfitted to be steerable, the industry of tomorrow will owe a great debt to the continually expanding knowledge gained from the efforts of a few dedicated balloonists.

Lighter-than-air science has a history which goes back centuries. Back in 1783, as Benjamin Franklin watched a French ascent, some skeptic asked him "Of what use is such a device?" Franklin replied "Of what use is a newborn babe?"

Today's airship is similar not to a newborn babe but rather to a Rip Van Winkle who has slept for forty years.

On a desolate wind-whipped hill near Palestine, Texas, one can hear the sound of men's voices speaking with British, German and American accents. These men operate the National Scientific Balloon Facility.

The balloons sent aloft range in size from 11,000,000 cubic feet (300,000 cubic metres) to 30,000,000 cubic feet (850,000 cubic metres), with much larger balloons scheduled for the near future. These vehicles are expected to rise 150,000 feet (45,000 metres) and carry a scientific package up to 100 days. Most of this work goes unnoticed, but without it, our broadening knowledge of cosmic rays, particle astronomy, optical, infra-red and ultra-violet astronomy and cosmic dust research could not be obtained. The glamorous flights are the rockets which put men on the moon or unmanned ships on nearby planets, but what could be a more glorious scientific success than preventing cancer caused by cosmic rays here on earth? These are the scientific missions of today's balloons.

As it stands now, the balloons are at the mercy of the winds. The jet streams are predictable, but there are some highly unpredictable wind currents above the earth's surface. The controllable airship would be used as a nearly stationary laboratory to obtain the necessary scientific data to aid the human race now. Because of the unique qualities of the airship, the required scientific data could be gathered far more quickly than if all of the exploration is left to balloons.

There is unlimited potential in the field of airship technology. A scaled-down airship might some day replace many of today's family automobiles.

149

Scientists employ high altitude research balloons to gather data (Official U.S. Navy photo).

It would carry a family of four, cruise at 150 miles (240 kilometres) per hour, have a maximum altitude of 500 feet (150 metres) and Mom or Dad could fly-it-by-wire without assistance. It would be possible to activate a mooring device which would use a strong magnetic field when the aircraft was within range of any large metallic device on the ground and gently pull it down to a safe landing.

We now stand on the threshold of a new era of airship transportation. Everyone acknowledges that there still remains a great deal of research to be done. Cost and performance characteristics are needed either to capture rôles now performed by other vehicles or to carve out new unique applications. Market research must parallel continued technical investigations of new concepts. Finally to attain full potential, the government and private industry have to become a unified team in this great adventure. When this finally happens, the world will once again hear the old familiar command, "UP SHIP!"

Santos-Dumont aboard his airship "No. 9."

lta glossary

Air Scoop: A channel for air to enter the ballonets.

Airship: Any lighter-than-air vehicle that is steerable and powered.

Air Valves: Valves which regulate the air within the ballonets.

Altimeter: An instrument for measuring the height above the earth's surface; actually a barometer measuring air pressure graduated to give altitude in feet or metres. Modern LTA vehicles would also use radio and radar altimeters.

Automatic Valves: Spring-loaded valves in the bottom of a gas cell which open automatically whenever the internal pressure substantially exceeds the external pressure, as when an airship with full gas cells ascends to a higher altitude, causing the gas to expand.

Axial Cable: A stranded wire cable running through the gas cells from bow to stern of the ship and connecting the wire bracing of all the main rings at their centers, reducing the loads on the framework if there was unequal pressure between adjacent cells.

Axial Gangway: This serves the same purpose as the axial cable. However, this is a girderwork structure that permits access to the gas valves and cells.

Ballast: Droppable weights used to enable the airship to ascend to higher altitudes or to compensate for gas loss or increased loads on the ship.

Ballast Recovery System: To avoid valving scarce and expensive helium, as the airship becomes lighter through consumption of fuel,

U.S. Navy C-class airship.

the exhaust gases from the engines are passed through condensers hung above the gondolas in order to recover the water of combustion.

Ballonet: An air-filled compartment inside the main envelope which, kept under pressure by a blower or other means, maintains a constant pressure in the large bag, regardless of changes in the volume of the gas.

Battens: Supports to help maintain the shape of non-rigid airships.

Blimp: A non-rigid airship.

Block Time: Elapsed time to complete a trip from door to door.

Breeches: 550-pound (250-kilogram) sacks used to carry water ballast, four at each end of the ship to quickly lighten the ship at the bow or stern as in take-off or landing emergencies.

Bulk Tank: Tank used for fuel storage. Its contents could be transferred easily to the supply tank.

Buoyant Lift: The lifting of the airship by the gas alone.

Captive: A balloon restrained by a mooring tether line.

Catenary Curtain: A curtain-type support used with suspension cables in the envelope of non-rigid airships.

Ceiling: The maximum altitude attainable by the airship under particular conditions. Above this level, the airship is likely to suffer structural damage.

Control Car: Usually a small enclosed streamlined car where the commander, the navigator and watch officers with rudder and elevatormen fly the rigid airship.

Crew Station: The airships of the Thirties required men in position to move the rudder or release ballast. These were their stations, sometimes located a few hundred feet from the control cabin.

Cruising Altitude: That normal altitude where it has been determined that the airship functions best.

Deflation Port: The rip panel or envelope section removed for envelope deflation.

Deltoid: A lifting body concept which does not require a ballast recovery system.

Dirigible: A lighter-than-air vehicle that is engine-driven and steerable.

Docking Rails: The only mechanical ground handling aid used with German rigid airships until the *Hindenburg*; running through the sheds and for 200 yards (180 metres) out into the field on each side, the rails carried trolleys to which the ship was made fast so that it was prevented from moving sideways while entering or leaving the shed or hangar.

Dope: A solution of cellulose acetate in acetone, brushed on the outer cover or fabric after it was in place to tauten and waterproof it.

Drag Rope: A heavy rope tapered and weighted at one end that is used as recoverable ballast. It is one theory that this rope was struck by lightning or hit a power line in the *Hindenburg* disaster.

Drift: The lateral motion of an aircraft over the

N-class airship under construction in 1951.

ground, due to wind blowing at an angle to its course.

Duralumin: Name applied to a family of alloys of aluminum.

Dynamic Lift: The positive or negative force on an airship hull, derived from driving it at an angle with the power of the engines. This is a method of compensating for degrees of lightness or heaviness.

Echo Altimeter: This instrument, used in German airships, measured the true altitude above the earth's surface by timing the interval between a blast of compressed air and its return to the ship. This was similar to today's

radar altimeter except for the electronics in use today.

Elevators: Movable horizontal surfaces at the tail of the airship to determine upward or downward motion.

Elevatorman: Usually one of three men stationed at a position to move the elevators. His orders were received through a ship-type sound phone from the distant control cabin in the giant rigid airships.

Envelope: The rubberized fabric or plastic material that encloses the lifting gas.

Equilibrium: That point when lift equals weight and the balloon or airship is neither climbing nor descending.

Boarding the "Los Angeles."

False Lift: Refers to the venturi effect of the wind that causes the balloon to lift before true equilibrium is reached.

Fins: Vertical or horizontal stabilizing surfaces at the tail of the airship.

Fixed Weight: Total weight of structure and other permanent installations on an airship.

Fly-By-Wire: An electro-mechanical method of controlling the manoeuvring surfaces of the airship. The systems use electronic control with servo-mechanical devices to eliminate the need for on-station crewmen as used in the airships of the Thirties.

Free Lift: At take-off, it was German practice to drop about 500 pounds (225 kilograms) of water ballast, to give an equivalent ascending force or free lift.

Fuel Gas: A hydrocarbon resembling propane with a specific gravity the same as that of air. It was used as fuel and carried in gas cells in the lower part of the hull.

Gangway: see Keel

Gas Capacity: The gas content of all cells 100 per cent full.

Gas Cells: Containers for the lifting gas.

Gas Shafts: Shafts made of wooden hoops and netting, extending upwards between the gas cells and used to conduct hydrogen from the automatic valves in the bottom of the gas cells to the exhaust hoods near the top of the rigid airship.

Girder: Metal beams used to construct the transverse rings and longitudinal members in the structure which resist compression and bending loads.

Goldbeaters' Skin: Superb gas-tightness, together with light weight, was attained by lining the inside of the gas-bags with gold-beaters' skin, the delicate outer membrane covering the large intestine of cattle. Each animal yielded only one skin measuring not more than 39 by 6 inches (100 by 15 centimetres). Usually some 50,000 skins would be needed for just one large gas cell.

Gondola: Generic name for any car suspended below an airship, possibly derived from the fact that the early zeppelin gondolas were not only shaped like open boats, but were intended to float on the water.

Propellers of the "Akron."

Gondola Bumpers: Low pressure air wheels mounted under the control car and the lower fin to cushion the shock of landing.

Gravity Tanks: Fuel tanks permanently installed over each engine car to feed the engines by gravity. A crewman was responsible for keeping the tanks filled by hand-pumping fuel up from the slip tanks along the keel.

Gross Lift: The total lift, under standard conditions, of the gas contained in an airship; equal to the total weight of the air displaced minus the weight of the gas.

Ground Crew: The larger airships sometimes required 300 or 400 men to handle the ship on the ground. The *Hindenburg* used mechanical handling equipment and a travelling mooring mast. The *Los Angeles* needed 157 men whereas the *Akron* with mechanical equipment needed only 12 to do the job.

Guppoid: A partially buoyant airship (hybrid) with wings, STOL characteristics and a great load-carrying ability (Megalifter).

Helipsoid: A partially buoyant concept (a hybrid) making use of V/STOL capability, also great load-carrying ability, much larger than conventional cargo helicopters.

Heli-Stat: Partially buoyant (a hybrid) V/STOL concept, using a conventional rigid airship de-sign with existing helicopter dynamic systems.

Helium: The second lightest gas known. It is produced from a type of natural gas.

Helium Heads: An uncomplimentary name given to lighter-than-air enthusiasts.

Hybrid: Part airship and part heavier-than-air design, combining buoyant lift with aerodynamic lift.

Hydrogen: The lightest gas known to man.

Inclinometer: An instrument which measures the up or down angle of the airship.

Intermediate Rings: One or two rings spaced between the main rings to reduce bending loads on the longitudinal girders.

Keel: A triangular-section corridor running from end to end of a rigid or semi-rigid airship composed of the two bottom longitudinals of the hull and an apex girder.

Kevlar: A new tough fiber developed for industrial uses and found to be useful for airship construction.

Landing Ropes: Ropes stowed in the nose in hatches which can be opened by wires from the control car.

Longitudinals: The main lengthwise strength girders of the rigid airship.

LTA: Lighter Than Air.

Main Rings or Frames: The chief upright structural members of the rigid airship.

Manoeuvring Valves: Valves fitted in the tops of certain gas cells to enable the commander to trim the ship by releasing gas from one end.

MAV: Modern Airship Vehicle.

"Metalclad": Trade name for the ZMC-2 built by Airship Development Corp. of Detroit, Michigan.

Mooring Mast: Because wind conditions sometimes made it difficult to put the airship in its hangar, a mast was designed allowing the airship to be moored in the open.

Non-Rigid Airship: A pressure airship consisting of a rubberized fabric gas bag whose streamlined shape is maintained by gas pressure and from which a single gondola is suspended.

Outer Cover: The outermost cover of the airship, usually a rubberized material or dacron for non-rigids and duralumin for rigids.

Payload: That portion of the useful weight which earns revenue—paying passengers, cargo or mail.

Powerplant: The engines used to propel the airship.

Pressure Airship: Generic term including both non-rigids and semi-rigids in which the shape is maintained by gas pressure.

Pressure Height: The height at which decreasing atmospheric pressure permits the lifting gas to expand and build up a relative pressure inside the cells so that the automatic valves open and gas is blown off. Following ascent to a pre-selected height, the commander may ascend or descend to any altitude below this height without fear of releasing gas. This was an important consideration in flying a hydrogen ship through thunderstorms.

Propellers: Usually two-bladed and built up of laminations of West African and Honduras mahogany and American walnut with a walnut veneer.

Rate-of-Climb Statascope: An instrument which indicates to the elevatorman the rate of ascent or descent in feet per minute or metres per second.

Rigid Airship: An airship with a rigid frame which maintains its shape whether or not it is inflated with gas.

Rudder: Movable vertical surfaces at the tail of the airship, whose motion steers the ship to port or starboard (left or right).

Semi-Rigid Airship: A pressure airship with a

"Akron" at mooring mast, 1932.

rigid keel running the length of the bag, either suspended beneath it or constructed within the envelope.

Skin Temperature: The temperature of the fabric envelope.

Slip Tanks: Aluminum fuel tanks distributed along the keel, they can be also used in an emergency as droppable ballast.

Square-Cube Law: If you double the radius of a sphere, the surface area (and therefore weight) will quadruple while the volume increases eightfold. Applied to airships, this means that as they get bigger and bigger, they should get better and better in lifting capacity and operating economics.

Stall: In aircraft, a condition where an extreme angle of attack causes a loss of lift and the aircraft falls out of control. An airship could rise out of control.

Statascope: See Rate-of-Climb.

Static Lift: The lift of an airship without forward motion, due solely to the buoyancy of the gas.

Step Climb: A series of climbs and level-offs in ascent or descent.

STOL: Short Take-Off and Landing.

Streamlining: The shaping of a structure so as to cause the least disturbance while passing through the air.

Sub-Cloud Car: A small streamlined enclosure hanging in clear air half a mile below the German Army Zeppelin, connected by telephone with the control car, and used for observation.

Trim: When weights and lifting forces are properly balanced so that the center of gravity is located directly under the center of lift, the airship is on an even keel and said to be "in trim."

Trolley: A wheeled truck, pulled by hand and rolling on docking rails. Trolleys served as points for attachments of tackles made fast to the airship fore and aft (front and back).

"Up Ship": The traditional command given for the "lifting off" of the airship.

Useful Lift: The amount of lift remaining after subtracting the fixed weights of the airship from the gross lift.

Useful Load: The load that the airship can carry, equal in weight to the useful lift. Includes fuel, oil, water ballast, crew, spare parts, cargo, passengers and so on.

VTOL: Vertical Take-Off and Landing.

Water Recovery: A method of recovering ballast by passing the engine exhaust gases through condensers to recover the water of combustion.

Weight Empty: Total of fixed weights.

Zeppelins: The common identification usually given to any class of rigid airship which follows Count von Zeppelin's designs.

Zulu Time: The standard of time as designated at the observatory in Greenwich, England (Greenwich Mean Time).

Workmen attach fittings and inspect envelope inside N-class blimp.

acknowledgments

The author and publishers wish to thank the following individuals and organizations for their contributions of illustrations and information: Aereon Corporation; Airship Advertising Inc.; All American Engineering Company; American Institute of Aeronautics and Astronautics; Association of Balloon and Airship Constructors; P. Balaskovic; Nick Bennett; Boeing Vertol Company, especially John J. Schneider; Cameron Balloons Ltd.; Civil Aviation Authority, especially L. S. Edwards; Conrad Airship Corporation; Department of the Navy, Office of Information; Developmental Sciences Inc.; E. I. du Pont de Nemours & Company, especially F. Hamilton Fish, Jr.; Federal Aviation Administration; Sen. Barry Goldwater; Goodyear Aerospace Corporation, especially Lyle Schwilling; Goodyear Tire & Rubber Company, especially Thomas B. Riley; Owen Hall; Andrew Halushka; Institute of Heraldry, U.S. Army; Moe Luff; Irving Mankuta; Megalifter Company; S. A. Morgenstern; Sen. F. E. Moss; National Aeronautics and Space Administration, Ames Research Center; National Environmental Satellite Service, National Oceanic and Atmospheric Administration; New York Daily News; New York Public Library Picture Collection; Piasecki Aircraft Corporation; Port of New York Authority; Raven Industries Inc.; Sheldahl Inc., Advanced Products Division; Society of Automotive Engineers; Tucker Airship Company; United Fruit Company; Westdeutsche Luftwerbung; Thomas Wolfe; Congressman John Wydler.

Inside the Raven hot-air airship during inflation.

index